5-Word Prayers

LISA WHITTLE

HARVEST HOUSE PUBLISHERS
EUGENE, OREGON

Cover by Brian Bobel Design

Published in association with The Christopher Ferebee Agency.

5-WORD PRAYERS
Copyright © 2017 Lisa Whittle
Published by Harvest House Publishers
Eugene, Oregon 97402
www.harvesthousepublishers.com

ISBN 978-0-7369-7071-6 (pbk.)
ISBN 978-0-7369-7072-3 (eBook)

Printed in the United States of America

17 18 19 20 21 22 23 24 25 / VP-SK / 10 9 8 7 6 5 4 3 2 1

To my beloved papa, Crules Rosamore Cheek...

*a humble, quiet man who fed me apricots
when I was little and came to visit and
led us in this simple prayer before the
meal: "Bless the Lord, O my soul...and all
that is within me bless his holy name."*

I still remember that.

CONTENTS

Why This Book...

It all started with the best of intentions.

I am looking for the perfect prayer book for myself, having been recently convicted that I need more of it in my life. I've been in an intimate relationship with Jesus Christ since I was six years old, but as it turns out, my prayer life through the years has suffered from numbing daily normalcy and piling to-do lists. More often than I would like to admit, my time meeting with God has hinged upon my level of current crises rather than the pull of the heart. The logical conclusion is that I need a prayer book to help kick my prayer life into overdrive.

I find the perfect one, and on the day it arrives in my mailbox, I rip open the brown padded envelope, sit with my coffee, and begin to read. Introduction, chapter one, chapter two—I digest it all. Fifty-six pages in and I remain hopeful, but I can feel the excitement for a new read beginning to wane as another feeling is silently taking over: overwhelmed. I know this feeling well, as it is something I've felt many times as a grown woman, and never is it welcomed. I also know better than to throw the towel in on a book so early, but I am gnawed by the feeling of being *not enough*. I worry that the prayer life I so desperately want isn't reachable, because this particular book's formula is not something I will actually do. Yes, I sit with my coffee and I read an inspirational book, but I am not inspired or comforted, not convinced or strengthened or personally understood. Instead, I am bogged down by lists and 1-2-3s and "do it this way so your prayers will reach heaven." I close the book and never pick it up again.

That night, as I lay my head on my pillow in the cover of dark, I feel defeated. My prayer life will never be what I want it to be, I tell myself. I am never going to be a champion prayer warrior, the kind who can influence heaven to get things done. I am never going to have the kind of connection with God I want because I am not disciplined enough to follow the right formula. The really spiritual people will do that. I must face the fact that I am not spiritual enough, and I need to settle for the prayer life I have, small as it is. Even if I don't follow the perfect prayer book, I trust that God will still love me.

The trouble is, I have hard things going on in my life at the moment. I believe in the power of prayer. I understand that the spiritual battle of good and evil is fought on my knees as I come to God with earnest requests—which is why I went looking for the perfect prayer book to help me with a perfect prayer strategy. It just didn't help me at all. It overwhelmed me and left me more hesitant than ever to pray in the dark of night, on a night I so desperately need to do just that. If I can't pray well, maybe I should just roll over and go to sleep, I begin to think.

But I need God. If I close my eyes, the heartaches will only meet me again in the morning. So I pray the only five words I can muster: *I love you, Jesus. Help.* As quiet tears come down my face, something unexpected and sweet happens: I feel the presence of God in a powerful way. He feels near, nearer to me than I have felt in a very long time. I have prayed only five words, but it is as if I have moved heaven. God has responded to me. He didn't need me to follow a formula or list to bend His ear to listen to the burden of my heart. My cry for help was tenderly heard, and I can sense it.

I have thought about this night and the power of that five-word prayer many times since. It's not that prayers require only five words, of course, or any other magical number. What matters is the heart, not a certain formula or list. Jesus isn't interested in the spectacular, for the most dazzling prayer without soul is but a vapid wind. Through this sweet night with Jesus, my heart has been realigned with the truth about prayer and the importance of my faithfulness to it rather than my dependence on human tactics to impress Him or try to manipulate a certain response. I'm just to come to Him in humility and weakness, thank Him, love Him, and—yes—ask Him for the needs and desires of my heart. Even as I write these words to you, I find myself profoundly grateful for this stunning truth: Prayer is not about word count, but about heart intent.

More than ever, I believe in the beauty behind five-word prayers. I wrote this devotional book for you because I know that sometimes it can be hard to get started talking with God. You may be where I was—wanting to improve your prayer life and fearing you can't. Maybe you've read all the prayer books and feel disappointed because you haven't been as successful as you've wanted. Maybe you haven't been able to stick with the suggested formulas.

Perhaps I can encourage you with a few reasons I believe short prayers can still be quite powerful and why praying these brief five-word prayers may be a wonderful place for you to start in your prayer life.

First, **Jesus often prayed short prayers.** Not all of Jesus's prayers were recorded in Scripture, but many of the ones that were are short. Even what is often called the Lord's Prayer, the prayer Jesus gave to His disciples as the model of how to pray in Matthew 6:9-13, is brief:

> Our Father in heaven,
>   hallowed be your name.
> Your kingdom come,
>   your will be done,
>   on earth as it is in heaven.
> Give us today our daily bread,
>   and forgive us our debts,
>   as we also have forgiven our debtors.
> And lead us not into temptation,
>   but deliver us from evil.

Christ's prayers were often brief but packed with meaning and uttered in the most intimate, poignant moments: "Father, glorify your name," He said, submitting to God's plan for His death and our salvation (John 12:28). "My God, my God, why have you forsaken me?" He cried from the cross, just before He gave up His spirit and died (Matthew 27:46). Jesus's prayers had power, no matter how long or short they were. As we model and follow the life of Jesus, we remember the power of His brief, impactful prayers.

Second, **when praying feels hard, it is our tendency not to pray.** Many of us have become discouraged through the years because we felt we didn't have the perfect words to start talking with God. Some of us have tried system after system that promised us a good prayer life. When we haven't been able to make that system work, though, we wound up frustrated. Maybe we even stopped trying or decided to quit.

The truth is, we won't always feel like praying. There will be desert periods in our spiritual lives where we must persevere to pray—even when we don't feel like it, even when we don't know exactly what to say. We need no excuse to communicate with the great love of our life, Jesus Christ. How barren our lives are without the intimacy of dialogue with our Creator! But when we try to create a perfect system by which to communicate with God, holding ourselves to some impossible ideal or standard, we will be less likely to desire a time of prayer. As a result, we won't make the time for it or will avoid it completely. When we think about praying just five short words to God, we feel less overwhelmed. The simplicity of these prayers helps to open our hearts to what God wants to speak back to us.

Third, **prayer is less about talking, more about listening**. I will never forget my husband coming home one night after meeting with his mentor—a steadfast, passionate believer of many years. He recalled his mentor saying, "The older I get, the less I talk when I pray and the more I listen to God and what He wants to say to me. Lately, I just sit in my chair and wait for Him to start speaking."

I've heard this echoed in many mature believers through the years. I have been a Christian for more than three decades, and this practice is one I have adopted for myself of late. There is such power in the quiet, the still, the waiting on God for Him to minister to our hearts through wisdom and truth. He is the God of the Universe with so much to say, yet too many times I suspect I have talked over Him. Many of us have spent many hours talking to God about what we want and asking Him for things, and so we have missed out on what He had to say to us. And then we lament that we don't know what to do or don't feel like our prayers are being heard.

By starting a conversation with God through a simple five-word prayer every day, we open up dialogue with Him while not monopolizing the conversation. What a beautiful way to open up a prayer time with God: to say five brief words, be quiet and still for a few minutes, and see what He might say back to us in response.

Five-Word Prayers is not a magical new method, a secret to prayer I've just unlocked that I now share with you. It is not the way you must pray or a scriptural formula. It simply represents an aspect to intimacy with God that He showed me through my own feelings of inadequacy. During a dark moment in my life, He met me in five small, heartfelt words.

These 40 days of prayers are not meant to be the extent of what you say to God. They are meant to get you started when you don't know what to say to God. They are intended to be the spark, the catalyst, the beginning of a dialogue with Him. It is truly my hope and prayer that every day, every prayer, will be a powerful exercise in humble soul surrender in five small words.

And if you find, like me, that on that dark night those five words are all you can say? I believe with the right heart, it is enough for God. Your words are…

Precious.

Important.

Valued.

Tenderly heard.

And if I may, as a small aside…If you've never thought of journaling before, may I gently nudge you a bit in that direction? There's something about writing things down from our own pens that help crystallize an idea in our minds and help us retain it. My desire is that each five-word prayer will spark rich conversation between you and God. I pray that in that dialogue, He will reveal beautiful insights to you—insights you will want to document and remember.

Thank you for taking this 40-day journey with me through the five-word prayers. May the words be meaningful, may the prayers be sweet, and may they draw you closer to your Creator who loves you so much.

> Blessed Lord…
>
> Let me climb up near to thee,
>
> And love, and long, and plead, and wrestle with thee, and pant for deliverance from the body of sin, for my heart is wandering and lifeless, and my soul mourns to think it should ever lose sight of its Beloved.*

Yes, Jesus. Amen and amen.

---

* Arthur Bennett, ed., *The Valley of Vision, A Collection of Puritan Prayers and Devotions* (Carlisle, PA: The Banner of Truth Trust, 1999), p. 127.

Thank You for finding me.

*Though you are at the ends of the
earth, the LORD your God will go and
find you and bring you back again.*

DEUTERONOMY 30:4 NLT

Being found.

I'm not sure there's anything our fragile hearts want more.

To peek into our soul is to see our depth of need: to be known, to be wanted, to be sought after, to be found. It is no wonder we spend our whole lives seeking connections, hoping to be noticed and accepted just as we are. And it's no wonder we feel crushed by the constant loneliness. We wished for the connections. We wished to be pursued. We hoped to be wanted, and then we weren't. Our soul cravings are a place of fear and hope, barely whispered…because to acknowledge them is to admit that we have engaged on a quest with an endless longing.

Our soul cravings are a place of fear and hope, barely whispered...because to acknowledge them is to admit that we have engaged on a quest with an endless longing.

We have gone to great lengths to find the thing only God can give: security.

Rest assured, God has gone to great lengths too. To go after us. To find us. To bring us back again.

The Lord your God will go: That the God who holds the entire world in His hands would take the time to go on our behalf is breathtaking. Can you even believe how He comes for us? He's not passively waiting; He's in active pursuit. The degree to which we find something is always the degree to which we desire it. We are loved to death by this sweet, gracious, and furious love.

And find you: Only God would want us enough to go to the ends of the earth to find us. It's so personal, it makes my breath catch. I think of the Good Shepherd, Jesus, seeking after the one sheep who wound up lost (Matthew 18:12). This is a determination to find. This is passion. This is our God, who pursues.

And bring you back again: If it weren't enough that He goes after us or that He finds us, Jesus goes beyond and brings us back too. Back may be different for us. Maybe back is coming to God in the first place. Maybe back is returning to God after an intentional walking away. Or maybe back is our spiritual life slipping and finally being reawakened to our need to go all in with Him. Back suggests that in our place of being found, wherever that is, God will not leave us there. It is always the desire of The Great One to give shelter to the homeless. In whatever state we find ourselves, we are all homeless without Him.

I know, friend. You have been let down, and it's hard to trust again. But let me assure you, He is different. And isn't the promise of the security for which you've ached your whole life worth the risk of hope? I wouldn't ask you to hope if I didn't know for sure He would prove faithful by the character He's already shown. Just look at His track record. He is the One who not only created you (Psalm 139) and died for you (Matthew 27; John 3:16), but He also came back for you (Matthew 28). And in that place He waits for you to realize how much you need Him.

God has proven His desire for us over and over again. Never doubt that His pursuit of you will be thorough and fervent and endless. Others will leave and let you down, but He is not going away.

You may be far. Still, He sees you. He mentions you specifically: "Though *you* are at the ends of the earth." God is not about convenience. He's not about reaching out to only those who are near Him. He will turn over every rock for you, scale every mountain for you, find you in the dark prison of your life where you feel like no one will ever see your soul. You may be far, my friend, but it makes no difference to a God in pursuit with eyes only for you.

Trust that someone is looking. Nothing says you matter more than someone looking for you. That someone is Jesus. It has always been Jesus. It will always be Jesus. He will never stop looking for you; so if you are weary, stop running.

And count on this: You will be found. God won't give up on you. His arms are waiting and open, and even right now, they are drawing you into Himself. Only God can find us and pick up the broken shreds of our lives that have chipped off from all our wandering. Only He can gather those shreds and make a whole heart beat again.

We are never too far. We are never too spent. We are never not worth it. Our good Father goes after us and finds us and brings us back again.

Oh God, *thank You for finding me.*

DAY 2

Please give me strength now.

*He gives power to the weak and
strength to the powerless.*

ISAIAH 40:29 NLT

This beautiful yet complicated life brings even the strongest of us to our knees. Roles are taken away without our permission, jobs are lost, loved ones go to heaven and leave us here on earth…difficulties we may have anticipated, but still weren't properly prepared to face. Our human fortitude is no match for the hurricane winds of our daily realities.

Many days a desperate, searching heart has prayed to God, *please give me strength now*. We need God's strength to withstand the winds of life that threaten to blow us into a place of skepticism and despair. We've prayed it in the quiet of night, lying on a pillow that never feels soft enough to grant us rest. We've prayed it in our car, driving numbly down this street and that, sitting in the tall grass, watching children playing and wishing we could be so carefree, clutching our memories beside fresh graves, begging for our hearts to stop breaking the whole way through. Only the strength of God can console our weeping souls.

Only the strength of God can console our weeping souls.

The Word of God promises, over and over, to give us the strength we do not have in everyday life and great times of trouble. Of all of the promises in the Bible, the promise of strength is among God's greatest. He granted it to prophets and kings and humble servants like His very own mother, Mary. Without His strength, a lifestyle of bravery is not possible. Scripture assures us that even when our lives are spinning out of control, even when we feel powerless compared with our circumstances and the strength of others, God is ready and able to provide. We need only ask Him and trust in His capabilities.

So for our daily comings and goings, for our difficult trials and tests, may we always remember to lift our eyes, to seek the help we need, and to pray to the God of all power, who longs to help us where we lack…

Please give me strength now.

I love You, Jesus. Help.

*I lift up my eyes to the mountains—where
does my help come from? My help comes
from the LORD, the Maker of heaven and earth.*

PSALM 121:1-2 NIV

I love You, Jesus, help was the first five-word prayer I ever remember praying. I prayed it one night when I was at a loss for words, distressed over my lack of change and growth, struggling over the same things I've struggled with for years. Sometimes I loathe the sound of my own voice, praying the same stale prayers for change that aren't guttural enough for follow-through. I'm a grown woman, for goodness' sake, but some days I feel like a child. I say things I don't want to say. I do things I don't want to do. I behave poorly when I know better. I know all the calorie counts and still struggle to eat the right foods. My flesh is an albatross and daily I yearn to overcome it. So many things in my life have changed since I was a child, yet so many things have not.

We are a shared human race, so I know you feel my plight. We are a people of hoping and wishing and praying and fighting, trying our best and lamenting our worst. We have great days and weeks and even some months and years…and then the crash comes, and we are left feeling that all the good we experienced was just a massive fluke. We struggle not to slip into skepticism. It's tempting to worry away our days and fear ourselves into numbness. And in those real moments, it may be that all we can offer to God are five simple words:

Even in this moment as we struggle, we can lift our eyes to the God who loves us.

I love You, Jesus. Help.

Those words may be small, but I believe that they are just the same as if they were a spoken novel of all the best heart alliterations, He hears them and responds with all fullness and tenderness of a Savior's love. This simple prayer calls on heaven. It says to God that though our heart is full of love for Him, it is breaking over the frustrations the world is causing us. This prayer is an abandoned prayer. It is a needy prayer. It is a sweet prayer from a helpless child to a Father fully in control.

Even in this moment as we struggle, we can lift our eyes to the God who loves us. We can lift our face to see Him in the dark, lift our voice to call out to Him for help. He is tender to our struggle. He is ready to respond to the need.

I love You, Jesus. Help.

I want to hear You.

Answer me when I call, O God of my righteousness! You have given me relief when I was in distress. Be gracious to me and hear my prayer!

PSALM 4:1

Prayer is the perfect symphony of child seeking with whole heart and Father responding in tender attentiveness. This was God's plan when He created a way by which we could come to Him with our needs, expressions of love, and deepest laments. Hearing from God is powerful. That the great God of the Universe would respond to us is something never to be regarded as small.

Telling God we want to hear from Him is a precious declaration. It's different from needing to hear, because desire drives us differently, more purely than need. When we need to hear from God, we are likely driven by our confusion, our angst, or the pressure of our crises and pain. He responds without holding our circumstances against us, for the desperate heart touches His in a deep place. But wanting to hear from Him is a delight of a different kind to our Father. It is the prayer-thirst of the psalmist in Psalm 42:1: "As a deer pants for flowing streams, so pants my soul for you, O God." This is the intent of a child who longs for the company and counsel of the parent who loves him so. I can't help but believe that after all the times we have shut out the voice of God in our lives, the prayer *I want to hear You* is an especially sweet one to our Father's ears.

> *Prayer is the perfect symphony of child seeking with whole heart and Father responding in tender attentiveness.*

Sometimes we aren't sure how to hear from God, though we want to. I believe we start with this simple prayer from a clean heart, and in that beautiful heart intent, God responds in different ways. Our job is to be aware, open, and listening as God speaks.

Through our circumstances. Sometimes God will speak (figuratively) through our circumstances. We will hear Him as He guides us into a place or out of another. It will be a sense, a nudge, an overwhelming coming together of something that goes beyond mere coincidence.

Through other people. Sometimes God uses other people

to speak to us. Listen to the wise, godly people around you. Pay attention when someone you know who walks closely with God has counsel for you. Listen to sermons and music by godly ministers. God can and will use their words to speak to you.

During your own quiet time. Your relationship with God is deeply personal and precious. His desire is to speak to your heart through intimate, one-on-one time with you. Open your Bible and dive deeply into the Scripture. You will find Him there. Pray, which isn't just saying lots of words, but is also quiet meditation, focusing on God, and listening. God wants to speak to us. We must simply be still, wait, and listen.

Lord, today, now, *I want to hear from You.*

Show me truth and righteousness.

Stand therefore, having fastened on the belt of truth, and having put on the breastplate of righteousness.

EPHESIANS 6:14

The heart of God is for us to know with full awareness and insight the right, true paths to take in life that will lead to abundance. It is for this reason He left us His Holy Word, the Bible, our guidebook for life. In it He makes it clear that "his divine power has granted to us all things that pertain to life and godliness" (2 Peter 1:3). The posture of God is to show us truth and right living. The posture we must take is to ask Him for it in prayer and simultaneously seek it out as we dive deep into God's Word.

Show me truth and righteousness is a prayer of need and

desire for growth and godliness. When we ask for truth, we're asking for clarity and wisdom in unclear situations. When we ask for righteousness, we're saying we want to represent God well and live in covenant relationship with Him.* Truth and righteousness must be pursued and fought for, even as society seeks to pull us away. This is why Jesus so clearly gives instructions of preparation in Ephesians 6. He tells us to put on God's armor and then tells us exactly the pieces to wear. The belt of truth (to strengthen our core). The body armor of God's righteousness (to cover us). This is the way we gain the truth and righteousness we need.

> *Asking God for more of Himself is the wisest prayer we can ever pray.*

Show me truth: When we pray this, we are not only asking God to give us clarity and wisdom amidst the confusion of this world, but we are also asking Him to show us Himself, for He Himself is the truth. Jesus tells us, "I am the way, and the truth, and the life" (John 14:6). Asking God for more of Himself is the wisest prayer we can ever pray.

Show me righteousness: When we pray this, we are asking God to help us honor the covenant (the acceptance of salvation and entering into a personal relationship†) we have made

---

* N.T. Wright, "Righteousness," *New Dictionary of Theology*, David F. Wright, Sinclair B. Ferguson, J.I. Packer (eds), (Intervarsity Press, Downers Grove, Illinois, 1988) 590-92.

† Learn more about receiving the gift of salvation on page 153.

with Him. Some days, as life feels quite routine and casual, we forget that we have committed to a relationship with Jesus Christ, to deny self, follow Him at all costs, and lead other people to come into relationship with Him too. We desperately need God to remind us about what right living looks like, as our recollections are short. A prayer for righteousness is a prayer for greater likeness to God.

God, today, as I can become so easily confused by the world, tossed about by this opinion and that, and as I desperately need to know how to live right and honor the covenant relationship between us, *show me truth and righteousness*, please.

DAY 6

This is beyond my ability.

Now to him who is able to do far more
abundantly than all that we ask or think,
according to the power at work within us...

EPHESIANS 3:20

There is great beauty in the surrender of human limitation. Though our tendency is to wrestle instead of rest, Jesus calls us to the latter when it comes to our relationship with Him. We can't do it all. We aren't the answer to our problems. We don't have everything figured out. Talented and wise as we may be, there are situations beyond our ability to handle. This prayer is a powerful admission to make before a limitless God: *This is beyond my ability.*

Joseph was summoned by the powerful Pharaoh to interpret his dreams. Though he had been given the gift from God to be able do so, Joseph recognized that he couldn't pull this off within his natural abilities. In fact, Joseph told Pharaoh, "It is beyond my power to do this" (see Genesis 41:16). In these few words of acknowledgement of human weakness, supernatural power was unleashed. It is always the deference to a holy God that fortifies our frailties and draws on the strength of heaven.

> *It is always the deference to a holy God that fortifies our frailties and draws on the strength of heaven.*

Joseph continued: "But God can tell you what it means and set you at ease." This is the statement of a man whose soul has found rest in God. Joseph's example shows a beautiful balance: He accepts his limitations and trusts fully in what God can use him to do. And Joseph's story teaches us this as well:

1. **Though God gives us gifts, we stay humble.** God wants to use us. But let us never think too highly of our human abilities.

2. **We always operate under the assumption of limits.** Humans have limits. Minds are finite. Bodies age and die. But God lasts forever. It's good for us to operate in our limits and not see them as a flaw to overcome. We should be our human best while understanding our human best will still be limited—a most powerful perspective.

3. **We defer to God in all situations.** Jesus knows

all. Jesus heals all. Jesus solves all. He is the vine; we are merely the branches. Our task is just to depend on Him.

Acknowledging that a situation is beyond our ability is allowing our soul to experience the deep ministry of a faithful God to meet the needs we cannot. So whatever we are facing today, however we need God to move, however our humanity limits our achievements, may we rest instead of wrestle, trust instead of stress.

Jesus, take this, which we cannot do. *This is beyond my ability.*

I am Your precious child.

Now...you belong to Christ Jesus.

1 CORINTHIANS 1:4 NLT

Sometimes I read the Bible and portions of verses strike me in particular with their beauty. The few words, the short phrases that mean everything, change everything, define my whole life like these from 1 Corinthians 1:4 (NLT): "Now…you belong to Christ Jesus."

I grew up with a family who loved me and fed me, gave me a name and a proper place to live. But not everyone has wanted me in my life. Not everyone has accepted me and made me a part of their group. I've been turned away, shunned, gossiped about, and rejected, just like you. Nothing hurts worse than being misunderstood and rejected—except being known and rejected, and most of us have experienced the pain of both.

Being a child of God changes everything. He chose us, we

chose Him, and in that relationship we *belong*. We've been adopted into His family. This reality brings precious healing to a heart stung by human dismissal, sometimes over and over again.

We belong.

We are claimed and spoken for.

There is so much holy responsibility in this understanding...and nothing really to say in response but an acknowledgment: *I am Your precious child.*

We don't have to wonder if anyone wants us. No more wondering about our worth: We know for sure that Someone wanted us then, wants us now, wants us forever. We are His, and that bond is not going away. We can live with hope, peace, and security. Now, because we belong to Jesus, we don't just walk around flying solo, doing whatever we want. Being His child brings the bond of beautiful allegiance. He wants us; we want to honor Him.

> *What God has created He is invested in.*

We don't have to wonder if anyone will be there. In God, we have a Father who is never leaving us. Deuteronomy 31:6 promises that He will never leave us or forsake us. Throughout the Bible, He proves His commitment and staying power, His unending loyalty and love.

In one of the most beautiful passages in the Bible, Isaiah 43:1-2, He speaks with firm and beautiful reassurance:

> Fear not, for I have redeemed you; I have called you
> by name, you are mine. When you pass through
> the waters, I will be with you; and through the
> rivers, they shall not overwhelm you; when you
> walk through fire you shall not be burned, and
> the flame shall not consume you.

Could this be any grander? He's a sure thing. He's not leaving us; He's not walking away. In our darkest hour, in our greatest moments of need, we don't have to wonder if anyone will be there.

We don't have to wonder if we will be taken care of in the future. When we mess up, when people doubt us and push us away, when all seems dark and unclear, we need not wonder if God has a plan for our life. Jeremiah 29:11 promises that as children of God, He has plans for us, to give us a "hope and a future." What God has created He is invested in. That, my friend, is you. Wonder no more about your future. God is all in with you. Don't waste your life in a prison of doubt. God is fully invested in your future.

God, I love You. I belong to You. *I am Your precious child.*

Help me honor my life.

Whatever you do, do all to the glory of God.

1 CORINTHIANS 10:31

We were created from the very dreams and ideas of God, the Master Crafter, who has no shortage of plans and forgets no detail. Ribcages inserted with sovereign hands, eye color painted in perfect hue, gifts and talents implanted inside for each of us to discover and share. What will we do with this amazing life God has given us? His desire is that we should honor it.

Help me honor my life is a prayer from a heart that respects its worth. This prayer nods in humble acknowledgment to the gift God has given us—the life, the breath, the opportunity to exist without debt for sin. Mere existence doesn't honor our life. Walking through life numbly, ignoring our physical and emotional well-being, taking our days for granted, is a life disregarded. We were made for more. We weren't dreamed up by God to squander our life away.

When the apostle Paul reminds us, "Whatever you do, do all to the glory of God," we must remember that our doing is a direct result of our being. What you do, my friend, is an outflow of what you are saying to yourself about yourself, what you believe to be true, where you are in your relationship with God. What happens on the outside first happens on the inside, so honoring our life must start there.

> What happens on the outside first happens on the inside, so honoring our life must start there.

Know your worth and identity. If we do not understand our value as created children of God, we will never fully honor our lives. Read Psalm 139. Read John 3:16. Pick up your Bible and read it, my friend. God tells you in the pages just how valuable you are and how much He loves you. Read it until the words soak in and you know it deep inside.

Believe your life has purpose. We cannot honor our lives until we believe we have purpose. This belief will drive us even in those moments when we feel let down, afraid, and inadequate. When human emotions threaten to sideline us, we must believe in our purpose deep in our core. (*The Purpose-Driven Life* by Rick Warren is a great resource for understanding your life purpose.)

Get in right relationship with God. Often we don't honor our lives because we are not in right relationship with God. All the life-honoring decisions stem from there, so we must deal with this issue first, that our hearts may be right. If you need to come back to God because you've walked away, turn back to Him again in a posture of repentance (1 John 1:9). If you have never made a decision to accept His free gift of salvation,* start there to begin a committed relationship for the first time. Honoring life starts with getting a relationship right with God, a decision from which all other good decisions are born.

So pray today with gratitude, in everything you do, *help me honor my life.*

---

* Learn more about receiving the gift of salvation on page 153.

DAY 9

You are sufficient and good.

*God is our refuge and strength, a
very present help in trouble.*

PSALM 46:1 KJV

Enough is a word we don't use much to describe what we have accumulated in our over-saturated, over-indulged culture of abundance. We have so much that, ironically, the concept of enough is nebulous and far from our reality. But if we ever face the moment we don't have enough—if the job is lost or the food is scarce or the ends don't meet—we realize that not having enough can bring us to fear and desperation.

In a spiritual sense, we constantly reside in this "never enough" space without God. It is why His being sufficient is of epic importance; the sufficiency of God is the answer to every gap in our lives. He is enough when we long to be loved. He is enough when we look for attention in disastrous places.

He is enough when we desire more. In every circumstance and situation, He is sufficient, enough.

The psalmist writes of this sufficiency of God in Psalm 46, detailing the things that cannot stand up against Him and how His heart is always for us, to rescue and to save. The goodness of God directly relates to His sufficiency, for if He were not enough He would not be good, and if He were not good He would not be enough. A good God is "always ready to help in times of trouble." A sufficient God is "our refuge and strength" (Psalm 46:1 NLT). Other things will fall short of being good enough for us, but God never will.

> The sufficiency of God is the answer to every gap in our lives.

Sufficient...enough for our every need.

Good...ready to save us.

Sufficient...enough for the deepest desire of our heart.

Good...fulfilling to the depth of our greatest wants.

This God, our help, our strength, is eager to be all that we want and need. When we stop and think of all the ways He fills our lives in the ways other things can't, we cannot help but say, *You are sufficient and good.*

With You, life makes sense.

*Seek his will in all you do, and he will
show you which path to take.*

PROVERB 3:6 NLT

If I had a dollar for every time I heard a friend say, "Life doesn't make sense," I would, indeed, be rich. The losses, the injustices, the maneuvering that doesn't work despite our best efforts, our desires that seem good but never become our gain. We want our lives to make sense, but we can't understand why we face so many struggles.

With You, life makes sense is not a prayer of thanksgiving made by a perfect person. These are not the words you pray after every chip has fallen into place and every dream has been realized. That perfect life, without any hint of doubt or worry, doesn't exist. This life, after all, is not our eternal life. But when we trust in Jesus and commit to a relationship with

> *When we trust in Jesus and commit to a relationship with Him, we change the status of our temporary lives here on Earth.*

Him, we change the status of our temporary lives here on Earth. We go from question mark lives of confusion and disorder to declarative lives of purpose and peace. Life with Jesus is not a life without trouble (John 16:33). But life with Jesus is a life that makes sense, and that is the life we truly seek.

Life makes sense with Jesus because He has given us our jobs in life to do. With the Jesus life, we don't have to walk around wondering what our life purpose is. God, in His Word, has already told us:

> Go and make disciples of all the nations, baptizing them in the name of the Father and the Son and the Holy Spirit. Teach these new disciples to obey all the commands I have given you. And be sure of this: I am with you always, even to the end of the age (Matthew 28:19-20 NLT).

The Jesus-following job is clear: Make disciples.

Life makes sense with Jesus because we have someone guiding us. With God, we don't make a go of this life alone. I treasure this, for otherwise I would surely be lost without a compass. The beautiful benefit of a relationship with Jesus is that He leads us down right paths. Our job is to seek Him; His job is to show us which way to go. Life on earth will not always be smooth, but with the understanding that God is guiding us, we can rest in the great promise of Romans 8:28: "We know that all things work together for good to them that love God, to them who are the called according to his purpose" (KJV).

We won't have perfect lives. But with Jesus, we can always say, *with You, life makes sense.*

Praise Him for that today.

DAY 11

Thank You for carrying me.

Praise the Lord; praise God our savior!
For each day he carries us in his arms.

PSALM 68:19 NLT

Every time I visit the beach and see the sand, my thoughts flash to the poem about the two sets of footprints. In the poem, the unknown author's footprints are beside God's on a journey through life. In the hardest seasons of that life, though, there is only one set of footprints—not because God has abandoned His child, but because He carried her.

I set foot on the sand and make my own footprints. As I do, I think about my own journey. At times I've felt abandoned by God, but in the end, He was always carrying me through. And I quietly whisper the same prayer: *Thank You for carrying me, Jesus.* I know that were it not for His strong arms of love, I surely would not have kept going another day. The beautiful truth is just as Psalm 68:19 says: "Each day he carries us in his arms."

One time when I was little, in the midst of a painful earache, a very tall man named Mr. Charles (a deacon at our Baptist church) showed up at the hospital, picked me up, and carried me down the hospital hallway while I softly cried from the pain in my ears. We had been there for hours and nothing had worked to soothe my pain before Mr. Charles came. I'm not sure why being carried by Mr. Charles was the thing that made me feel better, but it did. All I can tell you is that he was big and broad, and I felt safe on the shoulder of his pinstriped suit being carried in his gentle arms. Somehow, being carried by Mr. Charles made the pain lessen in a way I can't explain, even to this day.

God picked you up, put you in His arms, and carried you—even at your worst, even when you resisted and tried to walk away.

The Bible promises that our God carries us like this every day. He takes our burdened, heavy selves upon Him and walks us through our hard days, our insurmountable tasks before us, our seemingly impossible roads still needing to be walked. We don't ever outgrow His nurturing arms, no matter how old we get. There is no cap on when He is through carrying us, and we never get too heavy. Every day, He is ready to carry us, again, willing and able to take on that job, again, even when we don't know how to ask. Beautiful Jesus. No one is equally strong and sensitive to us like our God.

My friend, think of your own life now. Imagine your journey, those times you may have felt abandoned by everyone else. Maybe that moment is now. Maybe you have even felt abandoned by God. God will never judge us for the way we feel, but He *will* ask us to lay aside those feelings for the truth of His Word and trust in Who He says He is. He has carried you even when you couldn't feel it or haven't known it. He carried you through that divorce. He carried you through when that person you loved so much went on to heaven. He carried you through that job loss and the struggle with your identity and the deep wounding you never thought you could get past. Praise Him for this. Love Him for this. God picked you up, put you in His arms, and carried you—even at your worst, even when you resisted and tried to walk away. That is a God worth praising and loving.

Caring, loving, nurturing God…*thank You for carrying me.*

DAY 12

Grant me Your great courage.

Be strong and courageous. Do not be
frightened, and do not be dismayed, for the
LORD your God is with you wherever you go.

JOSHUA 1:9

In our daily going to the grocery store, doing laundry, heading to work lives, we don't feel courageous. We feel ordinary, usual, doing the same thing with the hope of being strong enough to make it through whatever life sends our way. Life is laced with both the daily and the difficult, and in both we need the courage of God to live victorious and free.

Grant me Your great courage is the heart cry of frail humanity. God wants us to affirm our need for Him in our inadequacy of ourselves.

Even the best and strongest among us will at some point run out of our own supply of strength. A flash-in-the-pan moment of human bravery will not be enough to endure the

> Perhaps the greatest use of our time is not in trying to make ourselves braver people but becoming people more reliant on the God of all power and strength.

cancer treatments. Conjured-up strength won't be an adequate match for the pain of a lost child. God's courage is on endless supply, and our daily prayer should always include asking Him to give us that which we desperately need.

Courage is what enables a person to face difficulty, danger, pain, and uncertainty without fear. The truest and most lasting of all courage must come from Almighty God. Courage from God enables someone to do something she would otherwise be unable to do by engaging the mind, spirit, and heart.

1. *The mind.* When God gives us courage in our mind, we are able to fight mental battles, which are some of the hardest to overcome.

2. *The spirit.* When God gives us courage in our spirit, we have a sense of freedom even in difficulties, which gives us strength to move on.

3. *The heart.* When God gives us courage in our heart, we have a steady assurance and peace that keeps us strong for the journey.

Perhaps the greatest use of our time is not in trying to make ourselves braver people but becoming people more reliant on the God of all power and strength.

Let us live with greater gratitude for the promise of Joshua 1:9—the Lord is with us, ready and willing to supply us with all we need for both the daily and the difficult. And let us pray today the five words we need to fortify our minds, spirits, and hearts in this life: *Grant me Your great courage.*

DAY 13

Help me to forgive others.

*If you forgive other people when
they sin against you, your heavenly
Father will also forgive you.*

MATTHEW 6:14 NIV

Forgiveness is perhaps the greatest exercise of self-death a human will ever face. To open or re-open hearts that have been broken by injustice, to offer to another grace and love without their being worthy of it, is to deny our very flesh. When we forgive, we make ourselves vulnerable. We take a risk that the person will hurt us again…that we will feel like we let someone off the hook when they should still be paying a price.

And yet living with unforgiveness is a risk too—a risk that we will never have peace in our lives. This is, ironically, the higher risk.

In a culture that prides itself on getting others before they can get us, the practice of forgiveness is something that doesn't line up. But forgiveness is the key that unlocks the chains of heaviness on our hearts. It has been said, and it's true, that forgiveness is not for someone else. It is for us.

> Forgiveness is the key that unlocks the chains of heaviness on our hearts.

When we forgive, we free our minds. When we harbor anger and bitterness against another, our minds are consumed with thoughts about them. These thoughts take up too much room. We have less occupancy for the good thoughts that deserve our mental space, so forgiving someone cleans the rooms of our minds for the truths we want to bring in.

When we forgive, we can heal. As long as we stay in a posture of unforgiveness, our hearts will not heal. We will go on living with half a capacity to love or have joy or find peace. If we want to be whole people, we have to forgive.

Jesus can help us forgive when we feel we cannot. This prayer—*help me to forgive others*—is powerful because it is God's intention for us. It is what He Himself had to do when He was betrayed, spit upon, mocked, and sentenced to die on a cross. It is what He still has to do as we daily sin and daily ask Him to forgive us.

Forgiveness is bigger than making things right between us and another person. It is about making things right between ourselves and God. It is the way we live with ourselves without becoming consumed by hate and resentment. This prayer is the courageous first step to setting our souls free from pain we didn't ask for or deserve.

And in that space, our heavenly Father who sees and knows and loves us will help us do the hardest thing we have ever done.

Without You, I am nothing.

*I am the vine; you are the branches.
Whoever abides in me and I in him, he
it is that bears much fruit, for apart
from me you can do nothing.*

JOHN 15:5

The world screams, "You are enough," and we are desperate to believe it. But being enough is different from being worthy and valuable. We are beautiful people, flawed to the core, but deeply worthy of love and of priceless value to our Creator God…every one. Every human is important. Jesus has no favorites. So to say *without You, I am nothing* is not to say we have no value. This prayer simply says that by ourselves, we are unable to thrive.

We thrive by abiding in God. In John 15, Jesus teaches His disciples the lessons He most wants them to know—the last things on His heart before He is betrayed and taken to His death on a cross. This reminder to abide in Him is a life lesson the disciples will need as they find themselves separated from their Lord in the days ahead. It is a life lesson we must know too. To abide with God is to follow the ways of a Father who is higher. It will mean to stay with God, believing in His sovereignty all our days, forever and ever, amen.

> We are meant to be nothing without God, for it is God who shines in our inability.

The Vine is the real power source. The branches are valuable and worthy; they are the Vine's beautiful outflow. But on their own, the branches can't survive. They are nothing without the Vine, and their fruitfulness depends on their proximity to the Vine.

Were we able to maneuver through life without God, able to control our own fate and determine all outcomes, we would never rely on the perfect God who has the better plan. We are meant to be nothing without God, for it is God who shines in our inability. To spend our lives seeking to be something is to spend our lives in endless toil. No role will ever be as beautiful as the one we play with God being everything and us being nothing without Him. As we abide in Christ, we can be the glorious overflow of His love.

Worthy, valuable, connected to the Almighty God—this is our beautiful, important life. And in that space, we rest in not being enough because He is. For when we choose to abide in Him, we can easily pray…

Without you, I am nothing.

DAY 15

I need You desperately today.

*We do not have a high priest who is unable
to sympathize with our weaknesses, but
one who in every respect has been tempted
as we are, yet without sin. Let us then
with confidence draw near to the throne
of grace, that we may receive mercy
and find grace to help in time of need.*

HEBREWS 4:15-16

There are days when we feel we cannot take one more step, take one more breath, live one more moment. I have friends whose children have gone to heaven before they have, and they needed God to help them get up in the morning more desperately than anyone else I've ever known. I've had my own desperate moments—moments in which I've known that if God didn't help me, I simply could not face whatever came next. We spend so much of our lives feeling desperate, whether we have created the hopeless situation or life has created it for us. It's why we behave quickly, respond irrationally, and try to run away from our problems. We are desperate to escape the pain, the struggle. We are desperate for peace, for acceptance, for wisdom, for joy, for fulfillment, and for real, lasting love.

> *He sees your desperation. He sees that soul hunger for love.*

Even the most powerful people in this world will one day be confronted by their inability to control all things. In that space, the only prayer is one of acknowledgment and surrender: *I need You desperately today.*

This is a prayer near to the heart of God. He knows. He was tempted too. He faced hard times too. He remembers His dark and desperate moments too. He became man so He could empathize fully with us in those things.

He feels. He felt the sting of betrayal and loss and suffering. There is no human emotion He hasn't also felt. In this, there is the deepest level of understanding no other human can adequately provide.

He sees. He sees your desperation. He sees that soul hunger for love. He sees all the dead ends where you've gone looking for it. He sees your tears over the broken heart and the suffering inside. He sees your loss and how desperate you are to rewrite history. Jesus sees it all.

What all of us desperate people need is the mercy and grace of God. We need His arms to hold us firm and tender. He is attuned to our prayers, ready to hear from us, and never more willing and able to respond than when He hears us pray these words: *I need You desperately today.*

Oh dear, desperate friend, in whatever way you can, pray it. He's there.

I'm sorry for my sin.

*If we confess our sins, he is faithful
and just to forgive us our sins and to
cleanse us from all unrighteousness.*

1 JOHN 1:9

Everyone loves a good love story.

The most cherished love stories are often the ones that involve a beautiful meeting, a breach in the relationship, and an epic coming back together—the coming back together being the sweetest, most important part because of the hope and beauty and restoration it brings.

When it comes to a relationship with God, words like *sorry* and *sin* and *confess* sit heavy with us. As we lament our mistakes, too often we view God in an aggressive, condescending role instead of remembering that even in His powerful authority, He is the great lover of our soul. Our relationship with Jesus is the one true love story of our life. The deepest, the most enduring, the most tender we have and will ever know. Anytime there is a breach in that relationship it has been a one-sided infraction. We will be the only one to ever walk away. Therefore, there will be an ongoing need for our gracious Father to take us back to be in right relationship with Him.

> Our relationship with Jesus is the one true love story of our life.

Confession—*I'm sorry for this specific sin* (which God knows, anyway, but wants us to acknowledge in order to make right)—and repentance—*I turn away from this sin and turn back to You, God*—is the way Jesus makes it possible for our love story with Him to be made right. It is perhaps the most important of all these prayers because it leads to your beautiful reuniting with your greatest love, Jesus.

When we say we are sorry with a sincere heart, God forgives us.* First John 1:9 is God's commitment to us on the subject. He tells us that in our confession of sin, our love story with Him is made right.

When we say we are sorry with a sincere heart, we are cleansed. So often we struggle with the part of our relationship with God that involves cleansing because it is our tendency to dredge things up again. To be cleansed means the sin is washed thoroughly, so that we cannot detect where it was previously soiled. Once that sin is confessed to God, He

---

* Learn more about receiving the gift of salvation on page 153.

forgives us and washes the sin away. For our relationship to move on, grow, and flourish, we have to let the sin die with the past. Our love story has come back together because Jesus says it should, can, and will, not because we deserve it.

So today if you are feeling defeated, ugly inside, bound by your bad choices, broken in your relationship with God, or maybe feeling like you never had a relationship with Him at all, remember that the greatest love story is the one you are meant to have with your Creator, God. He is waiting for you to come to Him today with a sincere heart and pray, *I'm sorry for my sin.*

I hold tight to You.

*Let us hold fast the confession
of our hope without wavering, for
he who promised is faithful.*

HEBREWS 10:23

The world is a swirling tsunami of fear, anxiety, pressure, and injustice, and daily we hang on for dear life. We look to our jobs to stabilize us, but we find that it's never exactly what we want. We chase the money, though it is never enough to push all the fears and problems away. Even the good things we cling to, like family, don't make us immune to the storms of life that thrash around us.

Those who survive life have learned to cling to God.

Let us hold fast: To hold fast literally means to stick firmly. Saying "I hold tight to You" is saying to God, "I will grab on to You and not let go." My friend, don't let go when it gets dark.

Don't let go when you think He's not doing what you want. Don't let go when it's stormy and you think you know a better plan for survival. Grab on to God for dear life.

The confession of our hope: Many of us want to have hope. We may even say we have hope or operate in life with short bursts of hope when things are going well. But to truly live with hope is different. This is a choice, a condition of the heart not based on circumstance. Holding tight to God is living with hope in the One we trust with our very lives—a trust that is never misplaced.

> *Those who survive life have learned to cling to God.*

Without wavering: No matter what anyone else says or what the world looks like, we stay with God. We won't waver; we don't doubt who He is. God gives grace for our humanity and struggle, yet His desire is that we hold to an unwavering reliance upon Him.

He who promised is faithful: God is a promise keeper. He is a faithful Father. When we hold tight to Him, we won't be let down. He will reciprocate our trust with stability and strength—all that we need for this life. His desire for us is not just to survive but also to thrive, and His faithfulness is to provide the needed life ingredients for both.

When we pray *I hold tight to You*, we tell God we trust Him with our breath, our sanity, our soul. These are precious words, powerful words—words that summon the Father to wrap heavenly arms around frail humans and hold us in safety and comfort as only our Father can.

I hold tight to You, Jesus. Amen and amen.

DAY 18

I will speak Your Word.

The word of God is alive and active.
Sharper than any double-edged sword,
it penetrates even to dividing soul and
spirit, joints and marrow; it judges the
thoughts and attitudes of the heart.

HEBREWS 4:12 NIV

For ten years I've been a speaker, traveling to different places, communicating crafted messages, sharing my heart. I speak about my faith, about the way Jesus changed my life, and the things He impresses on me to relay to others.

It's a beautiful way to spend my life, though not something for which I ever feel quite adequate. But in every situation, there is a moment in my speaking that feels different from all the rest. It's a moment that feels sharper, stronger, more powerful and present, as if the very air in the room changes. I know for sure—in a way speakers rarely do—that the message is completely resonating.

That happens when I speak Scripture.

There's a reason for this, and it's found in Hebrews 4:12. Because the words of God, the Word of God, is alive and active. Sharper than the sharpest sword, exposing your thoughts and cutting straight to your heart. Regular words can't do that. Words from human flesh can't deliver with such power. The prayer *I will speak Your Word* is a powerful commitment we make, not only to God, but also to ourselves.

The spoken Word of God has saved many souls from a rash moment of sin, a desperate moment of despair, and a bad decision that could have led to years of sorrowful regret.

We speak the Word to help others come to know Jesus. The Word of God is our go-to source for helping others come to know the Jesus we know and love. Its pages contain the story of His life and love, and how that love drove Him to die on the cross for each one of us so that we might have life abundant. Everything is in there, perfectly, for us to use to introduce the Savior of the world to those who have not yet entered into a relationship with Him. We speak the Word so others will come to know our God.

We speak the Word to encourage others in their daily life. All our best words won't heal like the Word of God. The greatest words of hope, comfort, wisdom, and grace are found in the Bible. So many times in my life, in deepest moments of grief for family and friends, I have lacked words that would comfort. But when I recall the words of Scripture and speak those to my hurting loved ones, a healing salve covers my void and eases the moment. Only the Word of God has the power to do that. (Sometimes we most need to speak the Word to ourselves, to speak hope and encouragement to our own soul first, that we might in turn encourage others.)

We speak the Word to remind us what to do. The spoken Word of God has saved many souls from a rash moment of sin, a desperate moment of despair, and a bad decision that could have led to years of sorrowful regret. In a moment of weakness and temptation, we speak the Word to draw on the angels of heaven to help us. When fear threatens to paralyze us or jealousy flashes in our face and we are seconds from lashing out, speaking the Word saves us from drowning in our sin. The steadied wisdom of the Word grounds us, time and again, reminding us of the way to walk.

Lord, as we go through this day, help us gather the strength that comes from this powerful prayer: *I will speak Your Word.*

That others will come to know You.

That we will be strengthened.

That we will remember what we are to do.

Amen.

You have been my God.

*You have been my God from
the moment I was born.*

PSALM 22:10 NLT

Sometimes the most beautiful revelations are birthed from life's most painful moments.

When David wrote the words *you have been my God from the moment I was born*, it was not an expression of thanks for an untroubled life. It was in answer to his own words of deep angst, frustration with God over current distress (read Psalm 22:1-9 to learn more). David did in this passage what he often did as he wrote: He was respectful but brutally honest with God about his laments, and then he was honest with himself about how much God was present in them still.

God wants us to approach Him the same way—with complete honesty about how we feel and offering our deepest sorrow to Him in the midst. He wants us to acknowledge to

Him—even in the moments we don't feel as close—how He has been our God, our creator, our lover, and our friend, as this revelation often comes through the fire of difficulty.

This simple prayer says to God…

…**You made me.** This acknowledgment of God's creation of you pleases Him as the master of a most exquisite piece of art. The creation of man could only be thought up by a Supreme God, and He wants us to recognize the intricacies of its genius. That He took the time to fashion you with your distinct DNA, gifts, and talents is an intimate act of a supernatural Father.

> Our relationship with Jesus is a long knowing.

…**You know me.** Our relationship with Jesus is a long knowing. No one knows you better. No one knows your thoughts, your aches, your longings, or your secret dreams. He charted the movements in your mother's womb, was there at the birth, and is present at the moment of your last breath on this earth. If we ever feel as if no one truly knows us, we can take heart and remember…God does.

…**You love me.** The simple words "my God" are breathtaking. My God is different from a god or the God. My God is beautifully up close and personal. How He wants us to know He is not far, not ever, but right with us every moment of our lives. He is ours; we are His.

Whether we are enjoying a moment of great joy and success

in our life or in a deep valley of sorrow, may we never forget our very personal God made us, knows us, and loves us in the most unique way we will ever know.

Thank You, Jesus, for *You have been my God.*

I welcome Your major realignment.

Create in me a clean heart, O God,
and renew a right spirit within me.

PSALM 51:10

Bold, audacious prayers can scare us, but it is the bold, audacious prayers we need to pray to see our lives change. In prayers like *I welcome Your major realignment*, we bow low, deferring to God's life-changing authority. To welcome Jesus to do His work in us is not just to say, "I won't resist You, God." It is to say, "I will turn the porch light on, be waiting with eager anticipation by the door to swing it wide and invite You in with open arms. And then, once inside, You do whatever You deem best to transform this place. I won't stand in the way, offer suggestions, or try to stop You in Your process. You, God, know what's best."

Most of us have to come to crisis points in life before we are willing to utter such strong, humble prayers. Yet were we to pray them regularly, let God clean us up and realign us daily, we would be the better for it. Psalm 51 was written after the prophet Nathan confronted David over his sin with Bathsheba and subsequent sins to cover it up (read the story in 2 Samuel 11–12). David was in desperate need of realignment. His crisis point drove him to pen some of the most beautiful words in all the Bible:

> Create in me a clean heart, O God, and renew a
> right spirit within me.

This petition for change has echoed from the lips of believers every day since. But do we truly count the cost of this prayer? If God doesn't shift things in us, we remain woefully the same. There is nothing as maddening as the constant drumbeat of a compromised life. As tough as it was, David experienced the rich payoff of God's major realignment. We can experience that payoff too.

If God doesn't shift things in us, we remain woefully the same. There is nothing as maddening as the constant drumbeat of a compromised life.

A major realignment means God will clean us up. This is the best news for those of us who have lived in the disarray of our own messes.

When God does a cleaning, it is thorough and sure, and the heart is where it rightfully centers. While so often we clean everywhere else, sweeping around, tidying up the outside to make it look good while hiding things in dark corners of the heart, Jesus gets to the deep cleaning, where it matters the most. When God cleans us up, He cleans us out of the things that are silently destroying us. He loves us too much to let private, festering sins take us down.

A major realignment means God will make us like new. The rich payoff of a bold, audacious prayer is the renewal it brings. When we welcome God in to realign our lives, we welcome a freshness in our spirit that is tangible and sweet. During his major realignment period with God, David asked for his joy to be restored, and Scripture shows that indeed, it was. (Read his beautiful song of praise in 2 Samuel 22.) The realignment of God won't always be pleasant in the moment, but it will be well worth it. For in the midst of it all, He will still be faithful, loving, and good, and in the end, He will have shaped our lives.

Not just in crisis, but even in the ordinary day when sin lurks and the heart has gotten dusty and needs cleaning… Lord Jesus, *I welcome Your major realignment.*

This is not my territory.

Our God is in the heavens;
he does all that he pleases.

PSALM 115:3

We are manic controllers by nature, getting our hands into everything, pushing circumstances to go our way, adjusting the timetable to our perfect scenario. It's hard for us to imagine that someone else could have a better plan, and rarely are we willing to entertain even the idea. We want our way. Our path.

But then a circumstance comes along that is outside our ability to control. On that day, we are forced to lift our hands in a posture of surrender and admit, "I can't do this. I can't fix it. I can't maneuver this situation and make it right." Those are agonizing admissions, and it's hard to see how they could be called a gift. But coming to the end of ourselves like this is a blessing. A hard, deep blessing, but one that forces us to turn to God.

This is not my territory is the prayer of a heart that has reached that place. This prayer offers the confusion, the dead end, the disappointment, and the impasse to the only One who can sort through our muck. My mother taught me this prayer. Many nights, in the dark and with tears, she would hand over her tough day in a ragged offering of surrender. She would speak only a few words: "This is not my territory, God, and You're going to have to deal with it." And somehow, though not always in the way she might have preferred, He did. I've since offered my ragged offering in the dark of night with these words too. Each day I have so many things that are outside my territory that I need to hand over to God.

One of the sweetest gifts God gives us is the gift of His authority. We can't manage our lives by ourselves, and I don't want to handle everything, as capable as I may try to be. I want to let Jesus handle the things I cannot and at some point, I won't have a choice. We are covered by a God who cares for us without any motive but love and in this, there is great comfort and rest.

> *We are covered by a God who cares for us without any motive but love and in this, there is great comfort and rest.*

Today, may we take our hands off the wheel, cease our need to control, and offer God five heartfelt words of surrender: *This is not my territory.*

Help me to forgive myself.

There is no condemnation for those who belong to Christ Jesus.

ROMANS 8:1 NLT

It is an uphill battle for the human to forgive; perhaps the hardest fought is the battle to forgive ourselves. So much of our lives is spent in a prison of mental guilt. We regret the things we wish we hadn't done, the things we wish we had done but didn't, mistakes, misspeakings, rebellions that cost us dearly, and entanglements that we never expected to bring such painful results. Days pass in grieving, and nights end in regret, and prayers wind up sounding like broken records. That is, if we bother praying at all. Avoiding God often feels easier when guilt is our best friend.

Help me to forgive myself is an important prayer for the health of our heart and a restored relationship with God. When Paul wrote, "There is no condemnation for those who belong to Christ Jesus," he was on the heels of his own distressed confessions of the sin in his life. He lived with the knowledge of his failures, and he knew how often he fell short:

> I love God's law with all my heart. But there is another power within me that is at war with my mind. This power makes me a slave to the sin that is still within me. Oh, what a miserable person I am! Who will free me from this life that is dominated by sin and death?" (Romans 7:22-24 NLT).

Paul is conflicted by what often conflicts us. We desire to do the right thing—to love and honor God—yet our willingness to respond to the flesh so often pulls us back in. It is a maddening tug-of-war that leaves us breathless and battered. We become frustrated at ourselves and often overcome by the weight of our weakness. Why do we continue to bow to unfulfilling, momentary wants? The mental game, which is too heavy to bear, has but only one reprieve, and Paul knows it: "Thank God! The answer is in Jesus Christ our Lord" (Romans 7:25 NLT). In crying out to God for help, we are able to do that which our flesh prohibits. This, my friend, is the only road to freedom.

Forgiving ourselves is our responsibility to a God who expects us to make much of the lives He has given us.

Forgiving ourselves is important for the health of our

heart. When we carry the burden of guilt and shame, we cannot be thriving people. Joy cannot live in a burdened heart. Peace cannot dwell in a soul of regret. We will never experience true freedom while shackled to the sin of unforgiveness, even for ourselves. Small bursts of a good life may come, but it will never be the full and rich one we are meant to live.

Maybe you wrestle with guilt over the way you've parented. Those years have left you with deep wounds and holes that can take years of joy away from us.

Maybe you're haunted by lingering shame over a sinful past. Jesus has forgiven that sin but you can't wash it out of your mind. Those past choices are coloring your future.

We must be honest with ourselves and own our mistakes, and yes, we must come to God with repentance and confess our sin. But once those things are completed, we are to move on and live—by the grace and help of God—full and wonderful lives. This is the gift of the second and third and eightieth chances, given by a God so gracious. This new chance is not to be thrown away or rehashed or lived with guilt or shame. Forgiving ourselves is our responsibility to a God who expects us to make much of the lives He has given us. We can't truly move on without it.

Forgiving ourselves is important for a relationship with God. If God does not condemn us (Romans 8:1) and yet we continue to condemn ourselves, we are dismissing the truth of Scripture. God is the Highest and Greatest, so His call about us matters most. For us to make a judgment call about ourselves and hold it higher than God's call about us is a sinful self-focus. It is prideful to take our word about something over God's. This focus on our own forgiven sin leads to a cycle of mental angst that is hard to overcome. So, filling our mind with Scripture about how God has forgiven us is vitally important to our mental health and well-being. (Start with 1 John 1:9; Ephesians 1:7; Romans 3:23; and John 3:16.) We honor God when we forgive ourselves.

We've all sinned. We've all done numerous things we aren't proud of and wish we could take back. Looking back doesn't always bring joy, for mixed in with good memories from our lives are memories of actions we wish we could do over. I know. I feel them too. I have days that I desperately want to relive, believing I could get it right if given a second chance. But I must forgive myself for not being perfect. I must forgive myself for not having been there when I said I would, not saying the best thing, not behaving like Jesus in that situation, not living up to God's standard even now. It is the same for you.

Jesus forgives us. Jesus loves us, no matter what. There is no condemnation in Christ Jesus.

Oh, Jesus. Help us. *Help me to forgive myself.*

DAY 23

May my life represent You.

*Imitate God, therefore, in everything you do,
because you are his dear children. Live a life
filled with love, following the example of Christ.*

EPHESIANS 5:1-2 NLT

Some days, we are our best selves—serving graciously, loving our neighbors, setting aside our preferences and annoyances to behave well. And then there are the other days.

Anyone can squeeze out a few good moments. All of us, when the mood is right or a motive is at play, can be on our best behavior. Actions can perform without heart quite well in small spurts of faithfulness, benevolence, kindness, and love. But our life has to be about more than just managing to eke out a gracious day or two. Eventually, who we really are will emerge, and we will wind up exhausted in all our trying without true soul engagement.

Good people don't just happen. (Perfect people don't exist.) We who desire to be loving, gracious, kind, forgiving, faithful, good neighbors, friends, and family members need only remember that Jesus Christ is the guideline to follow in our everyday lives. When we pray *may my life represent You*, we are saying to God, "You lived perfectly. I mess up. Please help me live like You and never dishonor Your holy name." This prayer is music to a Father's ears.

When we become a believer in Jesus Christ and commit to follow Him, we take on His name.* It then becomes not only our responsibility but our great joy to imitate what He does. We will never be perfect as He is, but we must always be in a posture of emulating His character and heart. We will never go wrong when we emulate Christ. To represent His life is to represent the life of perfection, one who loves and gives and serves without selfish motive or temporary bursts of kindness. Faithful is who He is. Good is His character. From the beginning of time, He has never changed and never will. To model Christ is to model a sure thing.

> To model Christ is to model a sure thing.

Let us not seek to muster up good moments to love and serve and give, but let us seek to represent Jesus Christ better, the only Perfect One who ever lived.

Oh Lord, my life is not my own…I have committed to You so I can't make this about me but about something bigger. *May my life represent You.*

* Learn more about receiving the gift of salvation on page 153.

I will follow You forever.

I am the light of the world. If you follow me,
you won't have to walk in darkness, because
you will have the light that leads to life.

JOHN 8:12 NLT

Following God forever is not for the faint of heart. The journey is beautiful, it is worth it, it is the only life that matters in the end. But it is a life to be taken seriously because choosing a leader is serious business. We must have full trust in His ability to lead the way. *Forever* is of binding importance. It means a lifelong commitment. There is holy obligation in the words *I will follow You forever*. This is a vow of love and honor to be taken to heart by the one who prays it.

Jesus tells us how to follow Him. He asks us to be all in. We must deny ourselves in exchange for a greater desire to please our Father God, just as Christ told His disciples before He faced His death on the cross. "If any of you wants to be my follower," He said, "you must give up your own way, take up your cross, and follow me. If you try to hang on to your life, you will lose it. But if you give up your life for my sake, you will save it. And what do you benefit if you gain the whole world but lose your own soul? Is anything worth more than your soul?" (Matthew 16:24-26 NLT).

Taking up our cross is not the easy way, but it is the way He expects, and therefore it is the only way. We do what He asks; we defer to His plan. We follow Him fully or we don't follow Him at all.

And lest in that talk of surrender we begin to wonder if the journey is worth it, He reminds us of the great reward of following Him. "If you follow me, you won't have to walk in darkness," He says in John 8:12 (NLT). As humans, we can't see in the dark. We lose our footing, stumble, and fall. We take wrong turns because our eyes can't see the right one. So to have His light means everything. It means life is possible. Without God leading us, life is unable to be truly lived. God does not ask us to follow Him forever without giving us the beautiful benefit of Himself when we do.

God does not ask us to follow Him forever without giving us the beautiful benefit of Himself when we do.

Will we have to deny self and defer to Him in order to follow Him? Yes.

But will it be worth it, as He illuminates our path along the way? Yes to that too.

Father, today as I struggle to die to self and trust You with my life, knowing You know the best way, help me mean these words to the depth of my soul: *I will follow You forever.*

DAY 25

Your love is my joy.

*May you experience the love of Christ, though
it is too great to understand fully. Then you
will be made complete with all the fullness
of life and power that comes from God.*

EPHESIANS 3:19 NLT

To be loved by God is to know joy. The depth, the steadiness, the calm, the balance, the perspective…the fullness of a life settled by the encompassing love of God is too vast for words. A person who knows this settled life knows the meaning of true and lasting joy. Only the Father's love is enough to cover the cracks of our soul that threaten to thwart the process.

Your love is my joy is a prayer that praises God for how well He loves us. This prayer acknowledges how perfectly He fills us and completes our life. Our Creator longs to bring joy to us, His beloved creations, and when we tell Him how He has done this, it deeply delights His heart. He died for us, not just so we could experience salvation, but so that we could experience His love in our daily lives—walking with us, lovingly guiding us, leading us in the best way, nurturing us through difficulties, providing wisdom and peace and, yes, joy.

Sometimes we get so caught up in prayers of supplication, asking God for what we want or need, that we don't stop and pray acknowledging prayers like these. It's not that God keeps track of what kind of prayers we pray, tallying up the requests and acknowledgements, requiring us to follow a formula. His desire is always that we come to Him in humility, seeking with a whole heart. Word count doesn't matter. Polished speech does not impress.

Only the Father's love is enough to cover the cracks of our soul that threaten to thwart the process.

But getting in the habit of dialoging with God about things we love about Him, appreciate about Him, and what they specifically mean to our lives, is a relationship strengthener between a Father and His child.

We want our kids to ask us for things. We delight in giving them things. Yet when they tell us they love us and, specifically, how they appreciate us, our heart is touched in a deep way. This is the power of this prayer.

Today, let us be grateful for God's love. Let us be grateful for the fullness of life that comes with it. And let us pray and thank the Lord for the gift of Himself and all He brings.

Father, forever... *Your love is my joy.*

DAY 26

You are my only Master.

*Ye call me Master and Lord: and
ye say well; for so I am.*

JOHN 13:13 KJV

What we say and what we do must line up in order for our spiritual life to truly grow. When we pray *You are my only Master*, we are telling God, "Nothing is above You; nothing is more important than You. I will give up anything. I will go anywhere. I will do anything You ask me to do." When God is our master, we will honor His requests with full compliance, understanding that His role is to lead and direct, and our role is to be in service to Him. In this way, our lives show what our lips profess.

As Christ knelt to wash the feet of His apostles, He said, in essence, "Don't just call Me the master of your life; back it up. Do the things I do as your master and follow My example."

Jesus doesn't just want us to pray words to Him. He wants us to follow through with those words in our lives.

The trouble is, in our everyday, we often let other things master us. We are mastered by our jobs, letting them take too much of our time and energy. We are mastered by our schedules, letting them rule our days and nights. We are mastered by pleasures that have become addictions, and now we bow to phone screens and TV shows and other vices we cannot seem to shake. Jesus may even be one of our masters, but that is not enough. He wants to be our one and only. He wants our full attention and allegiance, not because He is a needy, demanding God, but because He loves us with a fierce love, and He alone holds the title that in turn helps center our lives.

> *Jesus doesn't just want us to pray words to Him. He wants us to follow through with those words in our lives.*

A master has earned his title. When someone masters something, they have overcome all obstacles, fulfilled all criteria, and accomplished what it takes to be in this power position. Jesus has earned the title of Master by being the Perfect Savior of the world. He has no equal in ability or position in heaven or on earth. He has overcome, fulfilled the promise of Scripture, and accomplished what the Father set out for Him to do. He has earned the title of Master in our lives.

A master handles things. There's an understanding of capability that comes with the role of a master, and those who cherish the covering will feel relief by this hierarchy and role rather than stifled by it. While the life independent from Jesus is often met by things mastering us, the life following Jesus as our Master is the one in which we find joy and true love and peace. There is no sweeter life than the one where Jesus takes care of business and we sit back and enjoy being in such capable hands.

Thank You, Jesus, and today, with my lips and life may I truly say... *You are my only Master.*

Set my burdened heart free.

*The Sun of Righteousness will rise with
healing in his wings. And you will go free,
leaping with joy like calves let out to pasture.*

MALACHI 4:2 NLT

Often the solutions to our problems come not through better, more effective life strategies, but in unexpected surrender.

When we are bogged down by our circumstances, we think we need to get more organized, become streamlined, learn to say no. When we are choked by fear, we dream of a utopia in which to escape. When we are harassed by the strain of difficult relationships, we spend our days on the chase of the perfect relationship, which we mistakenly believe will solve our deepest angst. Our heart is burdened on a daily basis, and we long to set it free by running away.

But Jesus offers us something lasting: healing and freedom

of the heart and soul right where we are. Malachi 4:2 promises us the sweet freedom our burdened heart cries out for… and yet, not in the way we might expect. Freedom is offered by way of surrender of the will. Freedom comes when we give honor and reverence to God. What else would a freed heart ever want to do but to shower the Freer with such tribute?

But with Jesus, the open space is ours.

The illustration of freedom in this verse—"like calves let out to pasture"—is not used by accident. Behind an iron gate for their entire young lives, calves are timid when the gate opens at first, not knowing anything but a life of restriction. But once they understand the open field, once their hooves hit the grass and they see the wide earth in front of them, they kick their legs and run with abandon. They are meant to live in the free, open space, and when they do, their hearts soar with melodies of unbridled joy.

We are meant to live in that space too, my friend. We live much of our lives behind the iron gate of our own choices—or the choice of another without our permission—not knowing the grass under our feet and the song of freedom in our hearts. But with Jesus, the open space is ours. When we give our love and allegiance to Christ, He gives freedom to us. What a beautiful, worthy trade—a lifetime of leaping and opportunity without restriction.

It is my prayer for us today that no matter what burdens us, we will offer up our trust to a God who can heal us and release us, praying these five beautiful words…

Set my burdened heart free.

May it be so.

You take care of me.

*Give your burdens to the Lord, and
he will take care of you.*

PSALM 55:22 NLT

I t is a precious thing to watch a person take care of someone else. I'm in a hard season of life right now with a terminal father, who has a central nervous system disease. But watching my mother care for him, daily, lovingly, with gentleness and grace, is beauty in the midst of the pain. She waits on him, covers him when he gets cold, feeds him, and does all the things he can no longer do for himself. This is sacrificial work.

There are all kinds of good, loving people in the world who will do gracious things for us—give us money if we need it, let us borrow a car, cook us a meal, and invite us around their table. But being cared for in this tender way, the psalmist describes, is of a different nature. It is a caring that only Jesus can truly give—benevolence and comfort of the deepest degree for a soul in pain from a heart ailment. Jesus is our caretaker in the darkest of days, under the most dire of circumstances, when no human caretaker could possibly meet our needs. To hand our burdens over to Him is the greatest exercise in love as He shoulders that which has become overwhelming to us.

Our strong Father reaches down with heavenly arms to cradle us in the coldest nights, wipe tears with fingers we can't see, take heavy burdens off our shoulders, and nurture our weary bodies back to health.

When we pray *You take care of me*, we acknowledge that God is our great caretaker, the One upon whom we are dependent. No one else will be able to nurture us in our great distress. Though we often think of God in roles other than a caretaker, it is every bit who He is.

He takes care of our hearts. Jesus will never hurt us, ever.

He takes care of our bodies. Jesus keeps breath in our lungs.

He takes care of our souls. Only God can heal from within.

This is the sweetest, most precious truth: God is our caretaker. Our strong Father reaches down with heavenly arms to cradle us in the coldest nights, wipe tears with fingers we can't see, take heavy burdens off our shoulders, and nurture our weary bodies back to health.

Oh Lord, You are a good Father. *You take care of me.*

I want to trust You.

*Every word of God is pure; He is a shield
to those who put their trust in Him.*

PROVERBS 30:5 NKJV

Trust is handing over our greatest possession—our heart—
and asking someone to honor and protect it. It's an intimate, frightening offering, especially in a world where
experience has taught us that trust is a risk. We've had our
trust tampered with, dropped, walked on, misused, broken into pieces. Handing it over again goes against our self-
protective nature.

Jesus is compassionate with our concern. He has seen our
heart being carelessly mishandled in the past, and He has
mourned with us over the injustice. It is why He asks us to
put our faith and trust in Him, the one who will not disap-
point (Romans 5:5) or ever have plans for us that are anything

but right and good (Jeremiah 29:11). He knows that, because of how our heart has been hurt in the past, we may not feel safe putting our trust in Him. But our desire to trust Him, communicated through this simple prayer, *I want to trust You,* shows our heart's intent. And He will meet us right where we are.

God keeps His word. We have known the sting of betrayal. People say what they do not mean and mean what they do not say. They spin things for their own benefit. So we have become jaded to the word of others. But Jesus is a promise keeper. He is the God of His word. There is nothing He will ever tell us that He will not fully commit to keeping. In this understanding, our hearts are forever safe with Him.

> *Jesus will protect our hearts as we offer them to Him.*

Jesus will protect our hearts as we offer them to Him. Proverbs 30:5 shows that God is like a shield. This image soothes our anxiety, assuring us that He can indeed be trusted with our hearts. A shield is a piece of defensive armor that protects and serves as a barrier between all that comes against it and its intended target. What a powerful vision of how our Father will go to great lengths to stand between us and whatever threatens our hearts! It doesn't matter how fragile your heart is or how it's been broken before. With Jesus protecting it, it is safe. Nothing will get through.

So whether or not we have all the words or know how the trust will come, may God take the intention of our hearts in this tender offering: Dear God, promise keeper, pure and true, protector of my heart, here it is. *I want to trust You.*

Thank You for knowing me.

I am the good shepherd. I know my own.

JOHN 10:14

I sat once with a friend who cried over feeling misunderstood. "They don't really know me," she said about the friend group who had shunned her. Amazing, how miles on the body do not change the inward frailties of the heart. I'm sure the women had their reasons for pushing my friend away. I'm sure to them, the reasons made sense. Her exterior was tough. Sometimes her organizational gifts made her seem bossy. She had been hurt, and that made her protective shield go up more often. But get to know her, really know her, and you'll find one of the most loving, generous souls a person could ever want in a friend. I once told her if I was stranded on a desert island, I would wish for her to be along because I knew she would figure out a way to take care of us. I meant it, because she would.

Not being known, being misunderstood, feeling like

people do not see who we truly are, is a place of deep wounding for many of us. Our hearts long for acceptance for our rough places. We don't want to go our whole lives wearing masks in order to get people to love us. We complicate our relationships because we change parts of ourselves in order to fit in... in order to find approval. And then we either regret our inauthenticity or we wind up not being enough anyway, and we find ourselves abandoned and broken by the experience.

> *There's nothing we can say or do that would change God's mind about us.*

Rarely do we find love without selfish requirements. Humans just aren't good at knowing people and loving them anyway. This is why our hearts will only fully find rest in the acceptance of Jesus.

No one knows us like Jesus. We hide our true selves from others because we feel too flawed, too tarnished, too unimportant or small, and because in the past when we have let people in, it has often led to hurt. We believe that if people knew all our baggage and struggles, we wouldn't be loved or accepted. But Jesus already knows the ugliest parts of us and loves us just the same. Our every thought, every step, every tear, every breath, every second of life, Jesus knows.

No one loves us like Jesus. Even in the healthiest, most beautiful marriages, the best human relationships between parent and child, the love of God for His children is unmatched.

It is holy and perfect and beautiful and without error or bias or change. There's nothing we can say or do that would change God's mind about us. He knows us completely and loves us with passionate abandon, all the days of our lives.

As John 10:14 so beautifully reminds us, our Good Shepherd knows His own, even in a world which may never truly know us at all. We can take comfort in this, in the days we feel misunderstood or rejected, as the sweetest words leave our lips to say to our God...*thank You for knowing me.*

What a gift.

I will cherish Your grace.

*For from his fullness we have all
received, grace upon grace.*

JOHN 1:16

The grace of God has been passionately heaped on all mankind since He spoke this world into existence. John 1 details it so elegantly: how He made all things in grace, gave things life in the light of His grace, and defied darkness in that process. The extent of His grace knew and knows no bounds, for it meant divinity taking on human form, coming into the world, facing rejection, and offering Himself for our salvation. Nothing and no one got in the way of His plan of grace for mankind—nothing then and nothing now. It is truly as John writes of this miraculous love operation: "From his fullness we have all received, grace upon grace."

Grace upon grace…upon grace, upon grace: This is the story of our lives. That Jesus would, with such intention, come and live and endure and dwell and offer is such an incomprehensible, holy offering. We live under the precious covering of grace every day, and yet nary a day goes by that we fully know it. That God lets us have air in our lungs. That He helps us in our time of crisis. So many days go by, so many things we mindlessly rush by, forgetting that were it not for the grace of God, we would not enjoy any of it. The fullness of God is the reason for such grace.

> *The extent to which we cherish the grace of God is the extent to which we deeply inhale the gift of life.*

I will cherish Your grace is a prayer to acknowledge the sweeping sacrifice of our Savior. We value it, esteem it, take pleasure in it as we go about our daily lives. The extent to which we cherish the grace of God is the extent to which we deeply inhale the gift of life. It is not enough to acknowledge the birthright. It is to spend our days in an attitude of hallowed appreciation for this grace that allows us to be here and press on. We grab on to His grace, taking hold of His grand love gesture. In essence, we grab on to Him, for He, Himself, is the gift of grace.

Father God, thank You for sending Your Son, for being the Light of the world, and for giving us the opportunity to be your child through a personal relationship with You. Thank You for the fullness of who You are. Today, *I will cherish Your grace.*

You are my great Hope.

You faithfully answer our prayers with awesome deeds, O God our savior. You are the hope of everyone on earth, even those who sail on distant seas.

PSALM 65:5 NLT

Jesus is the great hope of this world, the only hope in the world we've got. He is the hope that will not be crushed by the turmoil and confusion of the world. He is the hope that can silence our tumult and bring our souls to a place of peace and rest. When we pray *You are my great Hope*, we stabilize ourselves, for in this declaration we lift our eyes above the chaos. We rise above the swirling mess.

Psalm 65:5 strikes a tender chord in my heart. God is "the hope of everyone on earth, even those who sail on distant seas." Some of us don't want Him. Some of us don't even know we have floated away. Some of us purposely sailed off, charting our own course, waving wildly to Him as if to say, "See you around!" Some of us took off in the way we thought best, and now we're floating adrift, without direction. And still, He's the hope. Still, He's there for us. The faithfulness of God overwhelms me, one so undeserving.

God is our great Hope. He will be the One left standing when all the other things we clutched to stabilize us are gone. He is the anchor, the strength, the courage, the promise that yes, our life can get better; yes, we can move on. We can choose to keep sailing on distant seas, but that will only take us farther off course—to our own detriment. Staying close to Hope is the best thing we can do for ourselves as we maneuver the rough waters of life.

Staying close to Hope is the best thing we can do for ourselves as we maneuver the rough waters of life.

Jesus is the great Hope of this world, always and forever. He's all the hope we have, all the hope we need.

May this thought fill us with gratitude and move us to come in tight to His side, praying with a heart steeped in love, *You are my great Hope.*

I will honor Your name.

*I bow down toward your holy temple and give
thanks to your name for your steadfast love
and your faithfulness, for you have exalted
above all things your name and your word.*

PSALM 138:2

The name of Jesus is a sacred, powerful treasure. Though many have let it slide carelessly off the tongue, may we quake at such a thought, for it deserves the highest reverence. Jesus gives careful attention to the honoring of His name and those who call on it. We are told to bow low in submission to His name. The Bible says one day all will take this posture in humble compliance to God's will.

> God has highly exalted him and bestowed on him the name that is above every name, so that at the name of Jesus every knee should bow, in

heaven and on earth and under the earth, and every tongue confess that Jesus Christ is Lord, to the glory of God the Father (Philippians 2:9-11).

To say, *God, I will honor Your name* is to not only revere it ourselves, but to step forward as an advocate. It's a personal *yes*. We are to use Jesus's name in the way God intended—with honor and respect. A loving child of God will always desire to preserve the good name of the Father she loves so deeply.

> *Better to offend a thousand friends than dishonor Jesus by remaining silent about our commitment to Him.*

But honoring the name of Jesus also takes on the advocate role in the sense that we not only preserve it ourselves, but we protect it fiercely with others. Where the name of Jesus is being taken in vain, dishonored, and used recklessly, we are to become loving defenders of our Lord. Our job is not to become combative and volatile, but to firmly and graciously defend the character of God by letting others know the name of Jesus is sacred to us and we can't tolerate its misuse. While these moments may be difficult, God will give us the grace and strength to handle them with wisdom and love. Better to offend a thousand friends than dishonor Jesus by remaining silent about our commitment to Him.

As we preserve and protect the name of Jesus, honoring it above all else, God honors His children by allowing us powerful use of His name. This name is a gracious gift of God.

People have been healed in Jesus's name:

> Peter and John were going up to the temple at the hour of prayer, the ninth hour. And a man lame from birth was being carried, whom they laid daily at the gate of the temple that is called the Beautiful Gate to ask alms of those entering the temple. Seeing Peter and John about to go into the temple, he asked to receive alms. And Peter directed his gaze at him, as did John, and said, "Look at us." And he fixed his attention on them, expecting to receive something from them. But Peter said, "I have no silver and gold, but what I do have I give to you. In the name of Jesus Christ of Nazareth, rise up and walk!" And he took him by the right hand and raised him up, and immediately his feet and ankles were made strong. And leaping up, he stood and began to walk, and entered the temple with them, walking and leaping and praising God (Acts 3:1-8).

Demons have been cast out in Jesus's name:

> As we were going to the place of prayer, a slave-girl having a spirit of divination met us, who was bringing her masters much profit by fortune-telling.

Following after Paul and us, she kept crying out, saying, "These men are bond-servants of the Most High God, who are proclaiming to you the way of salvation." She continued doing this for many days. But Paul was greatly annoyed, and turned and said to the spirit, "I command you in the name of Jesus Christ to come out of her!" And it came out at that very moment (Acts 16:16-18 NASB).

Gratitude is to be spoken in Jesus's name:

I bow down toward your holy temple and give thanks to your name for your steadfast love and your faithfulness, for you have exalted above all things your name and your word (Psalm 138:2).

Requests are heard and honored in Jesus's name:

Whatever you ask in My name, that I will do, that the Father may be glorified in the Son. If you ask anything in My name, I will do it (John 14:13-14 NKJV).

The name of Jesus is powerful because Jesus is powerful. May we preserve this great gift. May we protect and cherish it at all costs. And may we say in humble submission, *I will honor Your name.*

DAY 34

My confidence is in You.

*I pray that God, the source of hope,
will fill you completely with joy and
peace because you trust in him. Then
you will overflow with confident hope
through the power of the Holy Spirit.*

ROMANS 15:13 NLT

Confidence is an admired, attractive quality, and to find someone who emits it in a world full of insecurity is a rare find. For one's true self to be secure in soul things—that money and popularity can't buy—is richness indeed. I want more confidence. I need more confidence as I walk through this life. I suspect you do too.

We can make all the money in the world, have everything at our fingertips, but that will not give us the confidence we need. Most of us know someone who has it all but has never known the contentment of a steadied, confident heart, resting in more than the temporal glamour of the world. How sad to go through life never feeling grounded. How we all need to trust in something bigger than ourselves.

A relationship with Jesus offers this. Romans 15:13 is my prayer for you as for me, that our lives will be filled with the real things, the deep things, that will carry us through hard times and help us thrive.

God, the source of hope: There is no human thing we can lean on to provide the hope we need. No amount of money can buy us joy. No outside beauty can fix the inner turmoil we feel. No house can be built big enough to insulate us from pain. Our hope has to be found in the eternal God who brings order to our chaotic world.

> *Our hope has to be found in the eternal God who brings order to our chaotic world.*

Will fill you completely: Being filled means the emptiness goes away. While we have tried to do this on our own, Jesus is the only solution that is not an empty quick fix to our needs, which constantly need refilling.

With joy and peace: Two things we want the most but often elude us: joy and peace. A relationship with Jesus brings with it the benefit of both, even in the midst of the difficulties of life.

Because you trust in Him: Inner confidence comes through an underlying trust in God. We are secure and grounded because of our identity in Him.

Then you will overflow with confident hope through the power of the Holy Spirit: The word *overflow* here suggests that we have not only all we need but also more than we need. How amazing it would be to have a beautiful, overflowing confidence that comes from within. Imagine what we could share with others if we exhibited that confidence. It is what Jesus promises for those who love and trust Him. He will always be the One to give us the strength, hope, and confidence. This abundance doesn't come from ourselves, but from God.

We won't always feel strong. Life will sometimes feel too hard, and we won't handle it perfectly. But when we trust in Someone bigger than ourselves, we can live grounded, peace-filled, joyful lives.

Jesus, today, even in the midst of everything I face, *my confidence is in You.*

I rejoice in Your greatness.

*May all who seek you rejoice and be glad
in you; may those who love your salvation
say continually, "Great is the LORD!"*

PSALM 40:16

t is a rarity to go through life with a sense of strength and confidence as a constant companion, yet this is the life that Jesus offers. His greatness—King of all kings, all-knowing God of the Universe, One who holds winds and waves in subservience to Him—is unmatched in scope and splendor. As a child of God, this is the authority we walk in and under.

Yet His greatness is not just one of epic regality. He is equally great in tender matters of the human heart. One of my favorite verses in all the Bible shows this stunning contrast:

> Thus says the One who is high and lifted up, who
> inhabits eternity, whose name is Holy: "I dwell in

the high and holy place, and also with him who is of a contrite and lowly spirit, to revive the spirit of the lowly, and to revive the heart of the contrite" (Isaiah 57:15).

For a minute, let this soak in. God, who is the greatest, above all else in this world, brings His greatness down to us, the sinners who have messed up *again*. He comes to us, the rejected, simple, everyday people in need of hope and grace and love. He comes to reawaken our spirits, refresh us, restore us to a place of health, and give us another chance. This is something to rejoice over, my friend. When we give our hearts to Jesus, we embark on a relationship of power and strength like we have never before known. The greatness of Jesus Christ is not just in His authority over winds and waves, but in His compassionate concern for every created life.

> The greatness of Jesus Christ is not just in His authority over winds and waves, but in His compassionate concern for every created life.

Nothing could hold Him back from coming to us. Our hearts are where He dwells, because love propels the Father's every action.

May we never stop marveling over this understanding. Our God is great. We are His children. His greatness is to our benefit. He tenderly cares for us as we walk in and under His authority.

Lord, may we ever be mindful of how great You are. Words cannot express it. You are bigger than all our offerings of love and appreciation. But today, take this small offering as a praise acknowledgment that no matter what circumstances may say, *I rejoice in Your greatness.*

DAY 36

Please give me another chance.

*But this I call to mind, and therefore
I have hope: The steadfast love of the
LORD never ceases; his mercies never
come to an end; they are new every
morning; great is your faithfulness.*

LAMENTATIONS 3:21-23

Second chances.

I have asked for so many from God.

I guess they shouldn't be called second chances, really, since I'm mostly on my eighth, ninth, seventy-fifth, and two hundredth, depending on the particular infringement. I've gotten a lot of chances to work on that stubborn streak of mine through the years, especially in my marriage. I've had ample chances to deal with my off-and-on shopping addiction when I've blown it yet again, and I've asked God to help me abandon the shopping cart and just walk away while in Target.

That God offers second and third and hundredth chances is one of the most beautiful aspects of His character of mercy and grace. It doesn't matter why we need another chance.

> *Anything good always comes from Him.*

That God gives another anything on top of the gift of His Son's death on the cross is incomprehensible.

Another breath. Another step. Another smile. Another kind word. Another blessing. Another opportunity. Another hope. Another reason to thank Jesus.

Another anything good always comes from Him.

Please give me another chance is a prayer that, if we are reading this right now, has already been answered by the very sustaining of our lives. Yes, we've been disappointed at times. God is not there to get us out of consequence if that is our goal with this prayer. But He hears and honors the earnest heart that prays these five words with the intent to change and walk forward through life differently.

The steadfast love of the Lord never ceases: The fact that God is a rock—a steady loyalist for all time—is something that ought to speak love to the depth of our soul. No one else has ever been so true, our entire life. That He loves us firmly, constantly, and without a time limit is proof of His constant gift of another chance, despite our failures.

His mercies never come to an end: Forgiveness, kindness, understanding, compassion…these are the things Jesus Christ offers to us. There is no other place on earth to find such thorough salve to the soul.

They are new every morning: Your second chance started this morning. And tomorrow morning there will be another chance and another the day after. We don't use this as insurance to behave poorly; we remember this when guilt over bad decisions threatens to swallow us up and overtake us into another day. Jesus is the God of another chance, and praise be to Him for that mercy and grace.

Maybe you're tired of asking God for another chance—you've asked Him so many times before. Or maybe you've starting taking advantage of God's grace and watering down the magnitude of the gift of second chances. Either way, the mercies are new today, and here's what I want you to know about another chance:

1. *The motive for another chance must be change.* We can't just want another chance in a quick moment of angst, to make the anxiety go away, to get our fix, to feel better or make someone else happy. We have to truly be committed to change, to get it right and walk in a new way. This is a commitment of the heart, one that will last past momentary regret, tangent, and whim.

2. *The method for change must be repentance.* If we truly want to change, we must seek God in a

posture of repentance. This is not legalism—a bunch of rules set by an angry God. It is how we can reconnect ourselves to Him once we have sinned. If we need another chance because we have caused a breach in our relationship with God, the only way back is through repentance.

3. *The future must look different.* Our futures look different if we make the choice to be different and with the help of God. We break out of habits and ruts by the determination, commitment, safeguards, and accountability we put in place— and through prayer. It's not that we will never again have to ask God for another chance, but we will lesson our tendencies to slip into old patterns by setting ourselves up for a different life.

My friend, God offers you, even today, another chance. Humble yourself before Him. Thank Him for His mercies and His steadfast love. And pray these five words with an honest heart: Oh God, *please give me another chance.*

I want You the most.

You are my place of refuge.
You are all I really want in life.

PSALM 142:5 NLT

Humans were made with the need to want, so our lives are spent craving. We want comfort—a full stomach, a soft place to lay our head, pleasure for our senses, things that make us feel elation or relief in the moment. We want approval—to be known and loved, accepted and lauded for both who we are and what we have accomplished. We want control—to know and understand both our future and our past. And we want to be blessed—to be rewarded for the good we do for others as we measure ourselves by the standard of humanity.

It's natural to want these things, as they are desires of the flesh we wear. But it is Jesus we are to want and crave the most. That longing goes deep within our core. Anything else we use to fill that craving will leave us empty. It is why money is never a lasting satisfier—nor are looks, fame, wisdom, or even the best human relationship on earth. At some point all that we have will not be enough to fill the deepest longing in our soul for God. (Read more about this in the words of King Solomon in Ecclesiastes 2. I also wrote an entire book about it called *I Want God*, available wherever books are sold.)

> At some point all that we have will not be enough to fill the deepest longing in our soul for God.

When we pray *I want You the most*, and we mean it, lesser struggles fall into place. This prayer changes what we fight for, what we love, what we chase, what we are willing to change. When we want God the most, we don't spend our life in a whirlpool of man's approval, always making decisions based on others. We don't worry about whether or not our actions will result in people withholding their love. Our relationship with God is built on trust and faith in who He is, not what we think He can do for us. This is the beautiful, blessed life: the one in which we want God above all other earthly things that can never satisfy.

May this be our prayer today, Lord, *I want You the most*. And may we mean it to our core, knowing You are truly the craving of our soul.

DAY 38

You alone can heal me.

Heal me, O Lord, and I shall be healed; save me, and I shall be saved, for you are my praise.

JEREMIAH 17:14

If I calculated all the hours I have spent trying to fix myself, make myself better, more improved, I would likely be overwhelmed. Much of my life has consisted of running from something I used to be or running toward something I want to be—but I can never quite seem to get there. I lament the struggles, wishing to finally rid myself of that hang-up once and for all.

I suspect you relate.

Maybe you have a self-improvement book sitting next to you on your bedside table right now, hoping it will have the answer you have been seeking for so long. Maybe you're involved in ongoing counseling with a professional. Maybe you've been texting a friend all day, telling her how desperately you want a healed heart.

We all want to get better. We all want to be free from the pain of our past.

No one but God can heal the depth of our heart problems. No book can tell us enough. No counselor, as good as they may be, can help us solve our deepest soul searching. (And I should note that I'm a huge proponent of good counseling.) As long as we live, Jesus is the only one who truly knows us, so He's the only one with the healing we need.

> No one but God can heal the depth of our heart problems.

Heal me, O Lord: God wants to make us well. Jeremiah wrote these words as a man of confidence in approaching his heavenly Father, not in shame over his past or with timidity over the ask, but with holy respect for what God can do. In the same way, Jesus wants us to ask Him to heal us: *not with shame over the past or timidity over the ask.*

And I shall be healed: It is this "I believe, God" response that acknowledges to the Lord that you know He can do what no one else can. Sometimes we've been praying for healing for a while and it hasn't come. Sometimes in our human skepticism and disappointment, we feel as though we won't get better. But we must take what we believe about God's ability and trust His heart and acknowledge His desire for our lives to move on with fullness and meaning. Even if God doesn't choose to heal our bodies, He will always heal our hearts, and that is the better healing.

This very day, may we ask the Lord to heal us, with the full confidence in what He alone can do. May we believe His heart toward us, that He wants us to live well and whole. And may we stop running to the other things to try to fix ourselves when He is and has always been our only hope.

Jesus, *You alone can heal me.*

I reach out for You.

*I stretch out my hands to you; my soul
thirsts for you like a parched land.*

PSALM 143:6

There are times in our lives when things look dark, and of ourselves, we are unable to find even a crack of light. Maybe your heart is desperately crying out for a reprieve from pain, and reaching for God seems like it may be the only way. It's true; it is. Whatever our angst, whatever eats away at our souls, whatever threatens our ability to have joy and peace in life, Jesus is the sole solution.

God hears this prayer *I reach out for You*, and He does not turn away from this cry of our hearts. There is desperation in this prayer, as it is the turning to God for help and hope. He responds without fail. There is intention in this prayer, and intention is something God always honors. There is an understanding that He is the one to save, and this is a holy requirement for the rescue to become complete. This short prayer has the power to spark life-altering movement, which is why our flesh fights against it. God is the first thing we should reach for when we are hurting. Yet He is often our last resort. Gracious God that He is, He is available without judgment in either space. Whenever we reach for Him, rest assured, He is there.

> Don't hold back when you reach for God. *Bring your most honest, guttural self to Him.*

Don't hold back when you reach for God. Bring your most honest, guttural self to Him. He already knows where you are. He can handle it, no matter how deep and dark it gets.

Come expectant when you reach for God. God never under-delivers. In fact, He does more than you could ask or imagine (Ephesians 3:20). You will never be disappointed with God, no matter how many other people have let you down in your life.

Be ready to change when you reach out for God. Come humble. Come open to hear, even if you're going to hear about hard things, things that need to be shifted inside you. Desperation brought you here, so do the heart work to honor that dark place so God can truly make you better.

When we reach out for God, we find the hope and peace our souls long for. May this be our prayer in times of both great bounty and in days of dark, desperate need: *Jesus, I reach out for You.*

Thank You for seeing tears.

*You keep track of all my sorrows. You have
collected all my tears in your bottle. You
have recorded each one in your book.*

PSALM 56:8 NLT

I imagine Jesus a lot. When I read the Bible, I picture Him with children on His lap, smiling and laughing as they touch His beard. I picture sandals dusty from walking, dirt under His nails from working with carpentry tools. I think of Him with sweat on His brow and a sober look of determination as He turned over tables in the temple. I picture Him pausing for the unloved, touching the eyes of beggars to heal them, riding triumphantly through town on a donkey. I imagine palm branches waved by a crowd crying, "Hosanna!" And I picture those hosannas turned to shouts of hatred as Jesus marched to His own death for the sake of love.

But one of the most precious visuals I have of Jesus is the

one the Bible describes in Psalm 56:8: "You keep track of all my sorrows. You have collected all my tears in your bottle. You have recorded each one in your book." What a beautiful picture: Jesus carefully collecting each tear as it falls from my face, putting it in His bottle, recording it in His book so He can keep track of the sorrow and pain in my heart. This was the promise for David then, as it is the promise for you and me now. Your tears—the ones you cried when you thought no one else saw—were seen by God. He collected them, took note of them, and was tender to your pain. Not one tear was wasted or went unnoticed.

Your tears—the ones you cried when you thought no one else saw—were seen by God.

So many heavy burdens we humans have, and the Lord keeps track of them all. Maybe you're overcome by a struggle beyond your ability to fix, by a prodigal child running far away from God, by the condition of the world, by sins and perversions you wish you could un-know, by lost jobs and health crises and injustices that make us feel we're losing our minds. God sees us in our days of tears.

Just last week a friend whose father has Alzheimer's told me: "I've been a daddy's girl all my life. Now my daddy doesn't know me anymore." I saw the pain in her dark eyes. This adult woman, a little girl no longer, heaved her shoulders as the tears fell in her lap, because love knows no age limit. I get it—my daddy is leaving me in his old age too. These things are deep and hard and our tears are our human bond.

And God, kind and compassionate Father, understands this the most. He is the most sensitive to our pain and struggle, most attentive to our need. There is never a moment that goes by that He does not notice, never a tear that falls that He does not see. When we cry with our friends over coffee, when we silently weep into our pillows at night while everyone is sleeping and our pained souls can't find rest, He is present in the pain with us. It's what He promises. It's the God He is.

So let us remember this today. And let us thank Him for this precious intimacy.

Father, *thank You for seeing tears.*

PRAYER OF SALVATION

I confess You are Lord.

If you confess with your mouth, "Jesus is Lord," and believe in your heart that God raised Him from the dead, you will be saved.

ROMANS 10:9 HCSB

Many of us know of Jesus. Many of us have heard about Him, been taught about Him, and know Him to be an important figure in history. Even more of us may not believe in God but believe in prayer, though we do not fully understand how it works or to whom exactly we are praying. But there is a vast difference between *knowing* about such things—prayer, God, going to church, practicing spirituality even—and being engaged in a personal, intimate relationship with Jesus Christ. It is a relationship that has changed my life, and it would be my greatest joy if this book were a catalyst for that powerful relationship to begin for you, this very day. It is my hope that as you read about this prayer of salvation, you will come to better understand what is so special about this prayer in particular, how it can beautifully change your life, and why it is the most important prayer you will ever pray.

This 5-word prayer is just as simple as all the others we've prayed together in this book: *I confess You are Lord.* Yet it is a prayer of the heart that changes everything.

It is a prayer of hope and transformation that comes straight from God's Word. Romans 10:9 tells us exactly how to enter into a personal relationship with Jesus Christ. But it's not just in saying these words that the relationship begins. It is the heart behind the words that matters most. We must believe and acknowledge that Jesus was not just a good guy, not just a positive social activist, but the Savior of the world, the perfect Son of God, who took on death for us to save us from our sins (2 Corinthians 5:21; Hebrews 4:15; John 3:16) and was raised back to life by God to live in our hearts now, forever (1 Corinthians 15:4; Acts 2:32; Romans 6:4).

When we humbly acknowledge this to God, understanding that we did nothing to deserve this ultimate sacrifice and accept the free gift, asking Him to come and live inside our hearts and guide our lives, He will be faithful to do just as we ask. That's what the prayer *I confess You as Lord* really means. He longs to do this. He has been waiting on us to come to Him in prayer and ask. In fact, He created us to enter into this relationship and enjoy a life of fellowship with Him.

We don't have to understand all the aspects of the Bible and its stories or even fully understand everything about our relationship with God to make this decision. As with any relationship, your relationship with God will take time to grow and develop. We just need to know we can't save ourselves, and we need and want God to be the Savior of our lives. At the moment we pray this beautiful prayer with a searching heart, Jesus will enter into a relationship with us and never leave.

And what will a life with Jesus look like?

> My soul, praise the LORD, and do not forget all His benefits. He forgives all your sin; He heals all your diseases. He redeems your life from the Pit; He crowns you with faithful love and compassion. He satisfies you with goodness; your youth is renewed like the eagle (Psalm 103:2-5 HCSB).

Just in these few verses God gives us reminders of what a life with Jesus truly looks like. Jesus will bring…

…**forgiveness for sin.** Daily, hourly, I am in desperate need of this.

…**healing.** Jesus alone is able to heal every wound of the heart, mind, body, and soul.

…**redemption.** Christ delivers us from our sin. He rescues us from that sin because we cannot rescue ourselves.

…**faithful love and compassion.** Jesus will love us no matter what. He will never turn us away, and He will be tender to the hurts we endure.

…**satisfaction.** Temporary fixes will never fully meet the needs of our heart, but God can.

These benefits alone are enough to turn my life over to God, for they are things I cannot muster up on my own. The Bible is full of additional promises of the benefits of being in a relationship with Jesus—peace, joy, patience, self-control, wisdom, kindness, compassion, among other things. Never doubt that this prayer of salvation is a prayer that will drastically benefit your life.

A relationship with Jesus Christ helps our lives make sense. All of us crave clarity in this confusing world. We aren't sure what to do, how to maneuver hard roads, which choice to make, and how to balance our insanely busy schedules. Most of us live without knowing our true purpose, and this is the longing with the deepest ache. *What am I here for? Where am I going? Why do I matter, and why do I exist?* These are age-old questions. We long to have purpose. We dream of making a difference. We beg to do more than occupy space.

Jesus never intended this kind of desperate life for you. He offers a stunning solution by giving you a relationship with Him. He says, "I have come so that they may have life and have it in abundance" (John 10:10 HCSB). The God who loves you is not satisfied with your living a stale, confusing, unfulfilled life. He longs for you to choose the alternative life, the one whereby He directs your paths and makes your choices clear.

While a life without a personal relationship with Jesus may be filled with spiritual strivings, self-help hopes, and periodic highs, without the grounding that an ongoing relationship with Him brings, these moments will fizzle with the next crisis life throws our way. Choosing to accept the free gift of salvation and enter into a personal relationship with Jesus brings solidity to a life otherwise blown about by life's changing winds. When we are tired of this way of living, we will gratefully turn to God for His better way. I choose a relationship with Jesus Christ because I choose a heavenly future. I choose a true and lasting hope amidst a world of chaos. I choose a relationship with Jesus Christ because it's the only life that makes sense.

A relationship with Jesus Christ is offered to us simply out of love. Jesus has no ulterior motives when He extends to us this free gift of salvation. He has no favorites; He does not pick and choose those with the best pedigrees or the ones with the squeaky clean pasts, and He will never turn anyone away. Jesus didn't wait for us to become cleaned up and impressive to come and give His life for us. In fact, "God shows his love for us in that while we were still sinners, Christ died for us" (Romans 5:8). He came for love. He was rejected and tortured for love. He died for us for love. That's it, that's all, the end. If you are looking for the catch, you won't find one.

Yes, accepting this free gift of salvation comes with the understanding that you desire to love and follow Jesus in return. That means that if your lifestyle is contrary to the Word of God, you will want and need to change to honor Him. But that is something you will *want* to do as your desire for Him grows.

As we mature in our relationships with Jesus, the goal is one of holiness and godliness—becoming more and more like Him, the one who is perfect. We are human, so we will never achieve perfection. But as we align our lives to become more like His example, we will take on more and more of His characteristics. People will begin to be drawn to His love and light inside us that is unlike even the highest level of human attractiveness.

Jesus loved us then, He loves us now, and He will love us forever. This will never change, no matter what we do. While even the best of human relationships fail us, our relationship with Jesus never will. Always remember: *He came for love.*

A relationship with God is a simple yet life-changing process. Out of God's vast greatness, He made this most epic life event a process simple enough for even a child. This, too, shows how much He loves us, for He longs for every one of us to have the same opportunity to turn our lives completely over to Him to use for His honor and glory and make much of the person He has created us to be.

The book of Romans in the Bible gives us a full picture of where we are as people before entering into a relationship with Christ, which is where you may be today. Maybe you know about Him, went to church as a child, or even consider yourself spiritual. But you feel you are missing the intimacy with God I have described. The first thing we all must realize and believe is the truth of Romans 3:23: "All have sinned, and fall short of the glory of God." We have to accept that we are not innocent. We have broken God's law, and we are messed up beyond our ability to fix.

And sin has consequences. It's been that way ever since the beginning, back in the Garden of Eden. As the Bible puts it, "the wages of sin is death" (Romans 6:23). Our sin should separate us from God forever. That judgment and separation are the natural consequences of our actions. We can't blame this on anyone else—the sin is ours. It is in our nature. And because of our sin, we could never hope to spend eternity with God.

But Jesus offers a gift—a glorious gift. He has given us an alternative to that death sentence. The gift? Grace. As He died on the cross, Jesus took our sin on Himself. He received the judgment for our transgressions. We were facing a dead end, but Jesus turns us around and shows us the way to an eternity in heaven with Him. There is no way to gain that eternal glory but through Christ.

While the world may say there are other ways to get to heaven and escape our death sentence, the Bible says there is but one way. Jesus Himself said, "I am the way, and the truth, and the life. No one comes to the Father except through me" (John 14:6). The full story of Jesus's life and eventual death on the cross is detailed in the Bible, and if you aren't familiar with the story, I would encourage you to pick up a Bible and read it for yourself. Jesus's birth, His public ministry on earth, and His death and resurrection are all detailed there for you to get a full and clear picture. That God would sacrifice His Son to save sinners who rebelled against Him? Too incredible for words.

Once we are willing to see ourselves as sinners, accept the sentence of death and eternal separation from God, and acknowledge the gift of Jesus's death on the cross to save us from our sins, we are ready to enter into a personal relationship with Jesus. This happens through a ready, submitted heart and a simple prayer. Jesus doesn't expect perfectly scripted words from us. But because He loves us and knows we need His help, He does give us some guidance on how to pray: "If you confess with your mouth that Jesus is Lord and believe in your heart that God raised Him from the dead, you will be saved" (Romans 10:9).

If you desire to enter into this personal relationship with Jesus right now, here is a simple prayer to pray:

> Dear Jesus, I confess You are Lord. I accept Your free gift of salvation. I ask You to take over my life and lead me from this day forward. Thank You for dying on the cross for my sins. Thank You for Your grace and forgiveness and the gift of eternal life.
>
> In Jesus's name, amen.

My friend, if you prayed that prayer in this moment and meant it with all your heart, it is with great joy and honor I say to you now…congratulations! According to the Word of God, "Everyone who calls on the name of the Lord will be saved" (Romans 10:13). So it is official: you are a child of God. Now you don't just know *about* God, you *know* God. You have an eternity set in heaven, and nothing can ever change that or take your relationship with God away. You will not be perfect, and you will still sin and still need to ask God's forgiveness for those things. But you will do that under the covering of a relationship.

> I am convinced that neither death nor life, neither angels nor demons, neither the present nor the future, nor any powers, neither height nor depth, nor anything else in all creation, will be able to separate us from the love of God that is in Christ Jesus our Lord (Romans 8:38-39 NIV).

Consider your new relationship with Jesus Christ a marathon, not a sprint. Expect moments of discouragement and trial, because we live in a real world and this is real life! Jesus Himself tells us in John 16:33, "In this world you will have trouble" (NIV). Being a Christian does not make us immune from hard things. But the second half of that verse is the rich promise of God despite our hard times: "But take heart! I have overcome the world." No matter what, Jesus will be with us. He will never leave us and will give us the peace and strength to face all things.

Like a runner, we pace ourselves, and as we train our lives to look more like Jesus's, we value faithful discipline over time more than short bursts of good works achieved quickly. Remember that "God, who began the good work within you, will continue his work until it is finally finished on the day when Christ Jesus returns" (Philippians 1:6 NLT). The work in you has started today, when you prayed this prayer. But God won't be finished with you until you are united with Him in heaven.

I'm excited for your new journey, and I am praying for you—praying that you will grow in the grace and knowledge of Jesus Christ for the rest of your life. It doesn't stop here. This is just the beautiful beginning. You have a wonderful life ahead of you, the best life you have ever known. Oh, my friend…there is so much about Him yet to discover and know. As you move forward, there are some things I believe will be most helpful to you as you seek to strengthen your relationship with God.

Spend daily time with Him. There is nothing that will help you build intimacy and trust in your relationship with Jesus more than to read your Bible and pray every day. However this works best for you, however you will be most faithful to this commitment, however you will be best able to focus— that's how your time with Jesus should look. I recommend you start by reading the book of John, a chapter at a time. The Internet has great reading plans to help guide you in reading the Bible, should you like a bit of guidance and structure. But the most important thing is to sit in a quiet place, open up your heart, and ask Jesus to show you things you need to know. He will be faithful to do it.

Get into community with other believers. As quickly as possible, find a local church. We all need the strength community offers, and nothing is more powerful than a shared belief. Your church should be a place that feeds and nourishes you, and it should also be a place where you can contribute for the sake of the family of believers. Your goal as a believer in Jesus is both to be mentored by a strong, older-in-the-faith believer and also to be mentoring others at some point down the road. So seek out a place that you can be spiritually fed and also serve. Join a Bible Study or community group. Gather with a couple of friends over coffee once a week in your living room, and study the Bible and pray. Whatever you do, seek out a community of likeminded believers and meet with them regularly.

Eliminate whatever keeps you from growing with God. Hebrews 12:1-2 puts it like this: "Let us throw off everything that hinders and the sin that so easily entangles. And let us run with perseverance the race marked out for us, fixing our eyes on Jesus, the pioneer and perfecter of faith" (NIV). Just like anything else in life, in order to have success, we have to get rid of the things that keep us from it. A relationship with God takes effort as well, and God wants our hearts to be fully engaged. This will mean changing habits. Some of the places you used to frequent may tempt you to sin, and some of the relationships in your life may get in the way of your choice to follow God. This will mean making hard choices. If we want to truly experience the power and richness of a relationship with God in our lives, we must do whatever it takes to protect and nurture that relationship.

Get involved in ministry. Involvement in things that God cares about brings us closer to Him and helps us develop our spiritual character. There are ministry opportunities all around us if we will open our eyes to see them. People are hurting and need a listening ear. People need food and clothing. People are hungry for the truth but don't know where to turn to find it. We need to be aware of those around us and ask God where He wants to use us to share with others about the saving knowledge of Him. We are always to be giving personal testimony to the decision we have made and helping lead others to this decision as well.

I'm so grateful you turned to the back of the book and read about this prayer. Even if you didn't pray the prayer for salvation today, I hope and pray you will make that decision in the near future. I know it is hard to trust in a God you cannot see. But I can promise it is a decision you will never regret. Having Jesus guide your life is the greatest security you can ever know—the deepest love you will ever experience. Even now, may His heart gently draw you in.

...

If you prayed this prayer of salvation today, I would love to celebrate with you. Please go to lisawhittle.com/salvationprayer and click yes on "I prayed the prayer of salvation" for some additional helps and resources.

Jesus is everything. It is the heart, the passion and the leadership approach of author and speaker, Lisa Whittle. Lisa is the author of six books including her latest, *Put Your Warrior Boots On*, and a sought-out Bible teacher for her wit and bold, bottom-line approach. Wife, mom, lover of laughter, good food, her fluffy dog, interior design, and the Bible, Lisa is a grateful work in progress. She resides in North Carolina, and you can visit her at www.5WordPrayers.com.

To learn more about Lisa Whittle or to read sample chapters, visit our website at www.harvesthousepublishers.com.

Also by Lisa Whittle

Put Your Warrior Boots On
You Can Be a Spiritual Warrior

Does it feel like the world has gone crazy and you're just along for the ride? From bombings to bullying, the world has us on pins and needles—afraid for our children, fearful for ourselves, worried that we won't have enough strength to stand our ground.

But you don't have to start brave to stay strong.

Inspirational author and speaker Lisa Whittle wants you to experience the joy and release of trusting in your Savior to help you live a God-ignited life. Find the tools you need to...

- confirm Truth and keep anti-biblical messages from misleading you
- develop passion for defending your beliefs without letting personal pride interfere
- outfit your days to support your faith so your dedication doesn't fizzle

There's no better time than this moment to put on your warrior boots and discover the fearless life you've been called to live.

I Want God

It is in the heart of every person to want God, but life gets loud and we forget Him. We get consumed by our problems, our desires, ourselves. We forget our first encounter with the Savior and how much we once wanted Him...the way we believed He could use our life...the fulfillment He provides that everyday life cannot.

A guidebook, a teacher, and a resource, all in one, *I Want God* brings rich simplicity to life-altering principles. With her signature boldness and raw authenticity, author and speaker Lisa Whittle inspires with bottom-line truth about what happens when life gets off track and how to find our way back to the God we want most.

To learn more about Harvest House books and
to read sample chapters, visit our website:

www.harvesthousepublishers.com

HARVEST HOUSE PUBLISHERS
EUGENE, OREGON